A HANDBOOK OF
ADVERTISING TECHNIQUES

A HANDBOOK OF
ADVERTISING TECHNIQUES

Tony Harrison

KOGAN
PAGE

First published in Great Britain 1987
by Kogan Page Limited
120 Pentonville Road, London N1 9JN

Copyright © Tony Harrison 1987

British Library Cataloguing in Publication Data
Harrison, Tony
  A handbook of advertising techniques.
  1. Advertising
  I. Title
  659.1'028   HF5825

  ISBN 1-85091-384-6

Printed and bound in Great Britain
Richard Clay Ltd, Bungay, Suffolk

CONTENTS

PART FOUR: THE INDIVIDUAL ADVERTISEMENT

PART FIVE: PLANNING TO GET THE MOST FOR YOUR MONEY

ACKNOWLEDGEMENTS

I should like to express my thanks to Bev Ennis of Ennis Associates, New York for permission to use his material on product and consumer positionings, evaluation of advertising and some of the techniques he has developed in budgeting. Similarly Ray Morgan of RMP has given me material which I drew on heavily in the media chapter.

Apart from such specific indebtedness, my thanks are also due to hundreds of advertising people who wrote, designed and thought out the many campaigns I have observed and learnt from over more years than I care to remember. While I don't pretend this list is complete, I am conscious of having received help and encouragement and support from Vic Bloede, Alex Brody, Michael Davies, Dieter Eichelmann, Harald Einsmann, John Jackson, Frank Harling, Al Hampel, Wolf Kramer, Rainer Malkowski, Dermot McCarthy, Richardson McKinney, John Usher and Hansjorg Zuercher.

INTRODUCTION

The aim of this book is to help you prepare more effective advertising with greater ease and speed and, most importantly, with greater *certainty*, than perhaps you have enjoyed before.

Developing advertising campaigns that work is never easy and this book does not pretend to take the hard, intellectual work out of the task. However my hope is to show you a battery of working methods that professionals have assembled over many years of trial and error, ways of approaching the problem that have been proved to work. They will work for you if you master them.

Most of the techniques and practices described here have been developed in the marketing and advertising of branded goods aimed at a large consumer audience. Your market is different, you say?

I suggest it is only different in its superficialities. In its essence it is the same. These basic principles learned in the consumer goods field have been successfully transferred to selling high-ticket items, selling investments, persuading people to contribute to charities, encouraging industry to buy industrial goods. They work because the essentials of human nature are the same everywhere.

But if this is so, surely you can discover these principles for yourself? Yes, of course you can, just as you have the potential to invent the wheel or differential calculus. But, disregarding for a moment the enormous waste of time involved in learning lessons that have already been learned many thousands of times before, experience has shown that success is the result of a careful, methodical and logical *progression* from first principles to the final campaign. Missing out steps leads to falsifying the whole edifice, and it is precisely this mistake that the non-professional (and, let it be said, many over-eager professionals) can all too easily make.

The plan of this book is, paradoxically, to get you to the desired objective by taking what may well seem a long way round. The non-professional usually starts off where he hopes to end up – and in most cases this is at the finished advertisement. He says, 'I need an advertisement for this special feature in so-and-so' (very often the advertisement is produced because a media salesman has been able to unload some special offer which may or may not be a good deal) and, starting with the blank space he has bought, he attempts to fill it with a suitable message.

Our method is much more long-winded – or I am afraid it must seem so.

We start out by saying, 'First, you must understand the environment in which your product or service exists, an environment made up of your product, the other products that comprise the market, and those customers that you and your competitors are seeking to impress.

'Then you must find a way to profile your offering so that it is seen as unique and desirable against its competitors. After all, in most markets today customers have a great choice as to what they buy, so why should they buy yours unless they are convinced that it is in some way better for them?

'Finally, when you have found this uniqueness, you must find a way of expressing it that ensures it is actually communicated in the jungle of noise that is today's media world and communicated to those people who are your predestined customers.'

It will be clear that this is a longer route than simply saying, 'Let's think of an ad.' It will also be clear that it is not circuitous, that none of the steps I have suggested can safely be ignored. Let us repeat those steps again:

1. Understand your product.
2. Understand your competition.
3. Understand your customer.
4. Develop a unique promise.
5. Communicate it effectively.
6. ...and to the right people.

I have often talked to businessmen in this vein and received the impatient answer, 'Oh, but we only want an ad to put in our local paper next week. We don't have the time for all that rigmarole you describe. It may be fine for people with big budgets but it's not for us.' I think this is a totally illogical response.

After all, these steps only ask for intellectual activity. They do not – unless they expose the need for some research – cost the business money. So it is only laziness rather than lack of resources that leads to doing a scamped job.

And a scamped job is potentially much more serious for a smaller business than it is for a giant that spends many fortunes annually on advertising. Whereas big companies may waste money on ill-considered advertisements (and they are just as prone as the rest of us to the ill-advised media buy and the message conceived as a whim), these usually only make up a tiny percentage of their total spend and arguably a sum they can afford to waste.

A smaller business cannot afford to waste a penny. But the kind of not thought through, illogical advertising activity we have described may be its total investment in advertising. No wonder that the corollary to 'We're not so big that we need to take all that trouble' is often 'Advertising doesn't work for us, we've proved it'.

Let us spend a few hours to see how advertising *can* work for you.

PART ONE

The Techniques
of Positioning

The Techniques of Positioning

CHAPTER 1

The Concept
of Positioning

Definition

The 'position' a product or service is said to occupy is the extremely simplified persona that the product represents in the mind of a typical consumer. It is the sum of those attributes normally ascribed to it by consumers – its standing, its quality, the type of people who use it, its strengths, its weaknesses, any other unusual or memorable characteristics it may possess, its price and the value it represents.

We begin this book advisedly by talking about positioning. A comparatively new concept pioneered by two American agency men, Al Ries and Jack Trout, it is fair to say that they named and systematised a concept that was quite independently struggling to be born at the time.

The communications industry had come to realise that commercial entities like companies and individual branded products had long-term personalities just like people. Just like people, certain companies and brands would be credited with being forward-looking and efficient while others would be seen as traditional, comfortable and trustworthy but not very adventurous. And still others were sharp and not to be trusted, while yet others were plain boring.

It should be stressed that these personalities were long-term. They had grown up in people's minds and, while they must have been sparked off by something the company had done long ago, they often had no factual and direct relationship to company actions that took place in the present. But just as the social personality a person has defines the limits within which he can believably act, so these brand personalities delimited the possibilities of the brand. A warm, traditional, feminine personality like Persil could very believably claim mildness to hands and would, almost without the point being stressed in advertising, be believed to be gentle to woollens, whereas a tough, masculine personality like Tide could not make such claims convincingly. All this, it should be stressed, seemed to be totally or largely independent of the factual, chemical composition of the two powders.

It was also understood that some brands were very strongly profiled while others had almost no character. Often, this was a concomitant of market standing – a very well-established product that led its market usually had a strong, clear personality, while a latecomer with few distinctive characteristics was seen as wishy-washy and ill-defined.

But this observation begged the question of whether clearly-profiled products become leaders or, by becoming leaders, brands gain in profile and distinctiveness.

Various researchers started 'mapping' these differences by measuring where the various products in a market were seen by the consumer on some key issues. This graphic way of showing semantic differences became popular and was certainly part of the triumph of the word 'positioning' to describe this phenomenon.

It then became clear that while products used to fall into these situations more or less by accident, it was also possible to define in advance the general personality you wished the public to ascribe to your product and – assuming you always followed the parameters you set down and avoided obvious internal inconsistencies – ensure that the product actually enjoyed this position.

The practice of 'positioning' was born.

Look around the world of commerce today and you will see that many companies and products are very clearly positioned. Coca-Cola is teenaged, ubiquitous and very American. Hofmeister is a lager that is smart and street-wise. Bisto is simple and tasty and old-fashioned, and kids have liked it for a hundred years. Guinness is a friendly, classless beer with a comforting warmth and a good sense of humour. BMW is the chosen carriage of the well-off manager who has retained his youthfulness.

There are four very interesting characteristics of positioning models and they have very large consequences for companies seeking to operate in the market.

1. Positions occur along parameters that are important to the customer and are essentially selected by the customer.
2. The positions in the market are usually oriented on the market leader.
3. Only a handful of brands, products or companies can be organised by the consumer into positioning models.

4. Positions are *not* simply the product facts, but they approximate them.

Let us look at these four characteristics and see what they mean for us.

The first, that the customer chooses the dimensions on which he sees and measures products, is very logical. These, after all, are maps that exist in the customer's head and for his convenience. He (or she) may decide to classify restaurants, say, on the dimensions of price, cosiness and the quality of the food. So one would be seen as costly but having excellent food but also as being rather haughty and unfriendly, another would have good food, be cosy and friendly but also be good value for money, while yet another might be seen as wonderfully cosy but serving abominable food whatever it cost.

Now, the consequence of this for the marketer is that you disregard the customer's classification at your peril. If you start a restaurant where the lavish decoration and the quality of the table settings are its special feature and this is a feature that is of no importance to the customer then it will simply be ignored and you will be classified (and probably do badly) along the same parameters as everybody else.

The second point is a corollary to the first. The market leader tends to form the customer's view of the market (or perhaps has become market leader because he reflects that view, who knows?). So when you attempt to break into an established market you will be seen on the leader's terms and measured on the scale he has established. This is why all copiers are seen as better or worse or in some way similar to or different from Xerox. This is why all vacuum cleaners used to be called 'hoovers' and their way of performing the task of 'hoovering' seen exclusively in terms of the market leader.

Most of the markets for branded goods are what the economists call 'oligopolistic', which means that they are dominated by a few major companies. Retail establishments obey the same rules since there is only a handful of each type of shop in the comparatively limited area in which we do our shopping, and increasingly many of these are national branded entities like Sainsburys, Boots, Next and so on. Industrial firms obey the same rules – within the industry they supply, there will only be a few supplying a competitive product or supplying it within an area that the cost of delivery makes competitive. Whatever business you are in, there will usually be a comparatively small number of competitors who are really competitors – you are not usually competing in a vast, global marketplace. The selective effect occurs simply because the amount of time and brainpower people are prepared to devote to each product

9

purchase decision is strictly limited. With so many different products and services to be bought and all of them clamouring for attention, the consumer·deliberately restricts his selection and simplifies his choice or he would never be able to come to a buying decision. The consequence is that if you do not break into the charmed circle that most people know and recognise and make their final choice from, then you will find life very hard.

This last point leads to the question, 'Are positions then simply the fabrication of advertising, independent of the facts of the case?' No, they are not. Positions are the consumers' *perception* of facts. Facts that have been simplified and organised for easy retention, facts that may perhaps have ceased to be facts but that still linger in the public's mind, facts that have been dramatised and rendered important by advertising. Be warned that if you have some totally new fact to offer that does not fit into this scheme, then you may find it very difficult to communicate.

This, then, is the world of positions. It is the world in which advertising works. You will have to find out how to make it work for you.

CHAPTER 2

What Determines Positioning?

There are four factors that determine the position a product holds in the marketplace and these are:

1. The product itself.
2. The company behind it.
3. The competing products and companies.
4. The consumers and their vision of themselves.

Obviously, your first step is to attempt to judge what position you in fact hold. Now, while this can be ascertained with research that varies from the fairly rudimentary to the highly sophisticated, it is also something that you can make a stab at with no formal tools at your disposal.

The product

You may very well not know what position your product or service occupies, but you can make a sensible guess at it by considering the four factors mentioned above. It is important you attempt to do it with maximum *detachment*, not crediting your own business with any virtues and strengths that the more impartial consumer might not credit you with. The other factor you need to bear in mind is the *consumer's point of view*. Generally the consumer looks at things as they affect him. He wants to know what products will do for him and how they fit in with his needs. He has little abstract interest in the way your product is made, for instance, unless this gives him some concrete advantage. The fact that you use better ingredients or processes is a matter of profound indifference to him unless this fact gives him some benefit.

This is a particular pitfall if your product is used for some ancillary purpose. For instance, if your product is packaging material in some form. You may lavish care and technology on it, but your customer simply regards it as an unfortunate but necessary expense and his customer bundles it into the dustbin as soon as he has unwrapped the product that came in it. It can be fatal to assume that your product has the same importance to your customers as it has to you.

Finally, the customer is short of time. He is not a specialist. This means he tends to look at every product classification in a rather prosaic, traditional way. Something genuinely new needs to be related to something which is familiar if it is to be understood. This is why the first motor cars were called horseless carriages, why the first radios enjoyed the name 'wireless'. New types of product are usually seen initially as variants on something which is known.

So your product (or service) will be seen as a member of a familiar class – even if it may not completely belong in that class, even though you may have attempted to differentiate it from that class. And it will be seen for what it *does* rather than for what it *is*.

The company behind the product

Products come from companies. And those companies have a history, they have other products, they may have executives who are known, they have a home, a nationality, a total ideology that rubs off on the product. This is something we are all familiar with. Consider, for example, the reputation that Japanese products had 20 years ago and the reputation (based on a factual and dramatic improvement in product design and technology) they enjoy today. Consider the different range of qualities you attach to beer brewed in Yorkshire and beer brewed in London. Or the rather exotic, upmarket attributes of a soup that bears the Baxter's label, as against the simple, good-quality-and-good-value feel that it would have if it bore the name Heinz. Consider the different price you might expect to pay, the different sort of service you would certainly expect to get for the same item bought at Harrods and Woolworths.

This matter of company origin is particularly important in the retail sector. Shops, after all, sell literally thousands of different articles, some strongly branded, others seen as the shops' own. The most effective retailers (and many of today's retailers are marketing experts of the first order) have managed to develop the profiles of their shops very effectively. Sainsbury's have developed an already strong reputation for food so that they are unusally profitable and unusually successful in their own-label products. Habitat has developed a specific style which manages to be classless in a way that other furniture stores are not. If your product is sold through outlets as strongly profiled as these, its characteristics will undoubtedly be coloured by theirs.

The Competition

It is instructive to compare share of market with what can be called 'share of mind'. In a typical market the market shares may look like this.

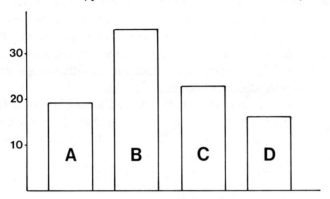

Figure 1 Typical market shares

The share of mind, measured perhaps by the frequency of spontaneous or prompted mentions in surveys will look much more like this.

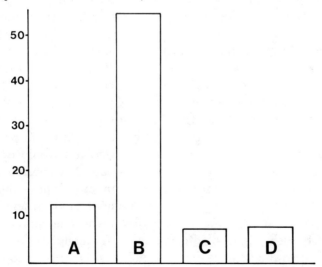

Figure 2 Typical 'share of mind'

The market leader in most cases has a much stronger share of people's minds than he has of the market. The market leader, in most cases, *is* the market in the eyes of the consumer. And if you find one of those rare cases where the market leader is not the most dominant brand in the consumer's mind, then there may well be an upset coming. This dominant effect of the market leader rubs off on all the other products in the market. For instance, if there is a clear market leader in the cigarette market, then other cigarettes will be seen as more or less strong than the market leader, as more upmarket or more downmarket than the market leader. If the market leader is a filter brand, then filter brands will be seen as the norm.

In the USA, Coca Cola and Pepsi Cola have such a stranglehold on the soft drinks market that the leading lemonade 7-Up was compelled to define itself as 'the Uncola' – such is the dominant and distorting effect of the market leader's position on the positioning of all other products. Harrods has such a share of mind as *the* upmarket store that stores that could easily position themselves in the top bracket anywhere else are forced to occupy a little lower position if they draw their custom from anywhere near Knightsbridge.

It is vital that you consider the competition, and particularly the market leader whose position in your competition is usually so dominant, when you judge the position your business occupies.

The customer

That the customer has a vital role to play in all this is something that has certainly emerged by now. The other three factors we have talked about – product, company behind the product, the competition – all have an effect on positions not so much for what they are but for how the customer sees them. Positions, it must be reiterated, are essentially *consumer perceptions*, rather than factual evaluations.

But quite apart from the fact that the customer's perception is key to all the factors we mention, the customer's perception *of himself* also vitally affects your position. If he sees himself as modern, progressive and up-to-the-minute he will be more demanding as to the progressiveness of your product. You will have to be very much in the vanguard of progress for him not to brand you as a stick-in-the-mud. If, on the other hand, he (and one should emphasise here that the pronoun 'she' could just as well be used and no discrimination is intended) feels himself traditional and with a taste for permanence, then he will be much more likely to view you as a Johnny-come-lately.

This would not all be so worrying if you could rely on the progressive element always to be progressive and the traditional element always to be traditional. However it is not so.

Consumers change their attitudes like chameleons depending on what they are consuming. We are all conservatives when it comes to beer – we want good, honest, old-fashioned beer brewed from country malt and hops and nothing else. When we come to buy a car, however, we want modernity and all the latest technology. We are severely practical when we buy down-to-earth, functional products like lavatory cleaners or washing machines and we don't allow notions of glamour to put us off the most logical choice. How different when we buy perfume! The subjective glamour of the product, the packaging, the name, the advertising take over completely.

Obviously you cannot evaluate the position your product occupies unless you have an inkling of how the consumer stands in regard to this product category and what type of character attributes are important in this category.

There is a way to judge this and it uses a very simple projective technique. You ask yourself what sort of person is the archetypal consumer of your product and also of the market leader. It is, of course, better not to rely simply on your own opinion. Asking the question formally of a number of consumers will always have more validity. But if the budget doesn't run to this, it is still better to ask the question.

The identity of the archetypal consumer is always a key issue in categories that a senior advertising man of my acquaintance described as 'products of conspicuous consumption' – cars, cigarettes, clothes and so on.

> The Mercedes is always seen as the proudest achievement of German
> engineering in its home country – but it has a worrying downside that
> comes from the observable fact that most taxis are Mercedes (and
> plodding diesels to make matters worse) and the car is the symbol of the
> tradesman (usually identified as a butcher) who has made his pile. It
> was this weakness in the overall very positive Mercedes position that has
> made it possible for BMW and Audi to do the seemingly impossible and
> make inroads into the Mercedes fortress.

The identity of the typical customer is so important in products of this type because when I buy such a product I identify myself with this mythical consumer. I say to the world – by drinking vodka martinis – that I am a particular type of person. And even though I may rather dislike the taste of vodka martinis and greatly prefer the taste of ginger wine, if the particular personality I wish to identify as mine is the vodka martini personality, then I will gulp them down and put up with the taste.

CHAPTER 3

The Position You Have, The Position You Want

Your position is so important because all else flows from it. It is, as we have noted, a long-term characteristic not easily changed. It is the basis of all your advertising and marketing activity and that activity will simply fail if there is a major fault with your positioning. The converse is that if your positioning is right, then the resulting activity, if it is in line with that positioning, will almost always be effective.

The first step, as we have said, is to identify the position your product currently occupies. You can define this by reference to your product, your company, your competitors and your consumers. These are the heights round about, and just as if you were trying to establish your position in a mountain range, by taking their bearings you can find out where you are.

The second step is to decide if your position is ideal. Since it will probably have just happened without any real planning it is unlikely to be so. You may decide that you are one of a comparatively large group of 'all others' with no distinguishing characteristics. Or you may feel you have got out of date, that your prime distinguishing characteristic is something the market no longer wants or finds relevant. Or you might feel that you have a strong and unique position but it is not capable of expansion, that you already have garnered all the business that your current position can give you.

Finally, a new competitor may have appeared that forces you to change the way your product is seen.

So you will probably want to modify your position in some way. How can this best be done?

The trick here is to make the smallest change necessary. If you can use your present positioning (or 99 per cent of it) and only need to communicate a slight but important shift, this is always far easier (which means far faster and far less costly) than attempting to change your position totally. Let us move out of the theoretical into the real world and see how this is done.

> The US car rental market was dominated by Hertz when Avis made their bid for growth with the advertising claim 'Avis is only Number Two in car rentals. We try harder'. As is common knowledge, this campaign was an outstanding success. Why? Because Avis had built on the position they occupied – a significantly smaller and less successful company – and made it a believable reason why one should try them. It was exploiting a position that existed (even if only subconsciously) in every traveller's mind. The advertising campaign was effective because it did not have to give people new information. It only had to communicate a new slant to information that was already known.

What are such elements of your present position that can actually afford a way to success? For instance, fortune could lie in your company's location. Perhaps, if you're located in the depths of the countryside, you can parlay that into a demonstration that your product is pure and genuine. Or perhaps that antiquated, outdated package you've always meant to do something about could be your way to fortune if you stress that the product inside is made with the honest craftsmanship that prevailed a hundred years ago.

Lucozade is an important product of Beecham Foods that has been established in the market for some 50 years. Positioned as a source of quick and easily assimilated energy, many years of advertising had stressed the brand's use in convalescence and, to achieve the strongest emotional pull in ads, had usually shown sick and convalescent children. This approach, while completely logical, seemed to stop building the brand in the early 1970s. Why? Analysis showed that there had been a number of changes in the health picture of the country. Many common children's diseases were now rarities and long convalescence had also become a rarity with effective, faster-acting drugs.

The fundamentals of the Lucozade positioning were still valid. But the stress on convalescence and particularly child convalescence were limiting factors and likely to remain so in a period of birthrate decline. Additionally, the stress on sickness in previous advertising was tending to confine the product's sales to the chemist's shop, whereas the grocery sector was growing much faster and was visited much more frequently.

The answer was not a change in fundamental product positioning but a total switch from featuring children and use in convalescence to featuring healthy adults and suggesting Lucozade as a frequent 'pick-me-up'. While the brand has not apparently lost its former franchise, it is now being used as a refreshing drink and not simply in

17

serious sickness. Grocery distribution and more frequent purchases have accompanied this shift in direction.

Of course, when a new product is introduced its positioning is much more fluid. The company's position will still have its influence on the new product and will shape attitudes towards it. But the product itself is a blank sheet of paper and its positioning can largely be determined. Even the company's influence will only operate if the company is identified. A lot of companies are so concerned to brand their new products strongly and effectively that they do not establish the company's ownership at all. Sometimes this is merely neglect. But at other times it is a deliberate policy. Procter & Gamble quite deliberately leaves the market to its brands, doing no more than identifying the company's ownership somewhere on the package. This is particularly appropriate if you are fielding brands that are deliberately competing with each other.

The first thing to appreciate with new products is this: *if you do not deliberately position the product where you want it, the market will. And it will choose the most obvious position.*

When Opel first launched the Ascona there was a kind of halfhearted positioning of the car as 'Not too big, not too small'. It had been developed as an intermediate model between the Kadett and the Rekord, but whereas the Kadett had stayed clearly in the small car sector, the Rekord had grown in successive models (and also in price), and there was a gap between the two that the Ascona could exploit. However, there was a problem. Ford's Taunus/Cortina model had firmly occupied that gap, and was clearly seen as the car that offered big car advantages at a low price. Since the market always saw GM and Ford as direct competitors, it accepted the GM model at its face value and identified it as smaller and less roomy than the Ford but priced about the same – an obvious loser's position.

Fortunately, the incipient problem was spotted before the car was really established – while the slate was still clean. The Ascona was positioned deliberately in the growing class of compact, sporty saloons. This meant emphasising the more powerful engine options and the more sporty versions of the car, stressing roadholding, acceleration and the fun of driving, putting the car in comparative tests with cars like the BMW 1600 and the Alfa Romeo Guilia Super where, while it might not have all their sophistication, it scored well for value and reliability.

This positioning was accepted and the Ascona went on to be Opel's (and under the name Cavalier, Vauxhall's) most successful model. The single issue of size and room where it lost against Ford had been successfully pushed into the background.

Looking at this instructive case, it must be remembered that the market positioned the GM car against the Ford simply because that was the behaviour they had learned. Everywhere, since time immemorial, GM and Ford models had been positioned in direct competition with each other. So the market as always took the most logical and most obvious assumption.

Launching a new product, even the category in which your product is positioned is to a certain extent up to you. Making sure you are seen in the right context is a vital part of optimising future sales.

When Kellogg's launched their Super Noodles product it was clear that they would have to find their business as an accompaniment to main meals – in fact, the traditional use of all pasta products.

However it was interesting to see how the conservative British took the obligatory starch accompaniment to a main meal. The total (and massive) market was made up as follows:

1977 £m.RSP

Fresh potatoes	475
Instant potatoes	19
Packet pasta	13
Canned pasta	33
Packet rice	25
Savoury rice	5
Total	570

In other words, the potato was totally dominant and the new product would have to take business from potatoes since the packet pasta sector in which it logically belonged was only some $2\frac{1}{2}$ per cent of the whole. The brand was launched with a TV commercial that used an animated potato as a spokesman and featured the claim 'Good enough to give potatoes a day off'.

Notice that Kellogg's did not try to attack the firmly entrenched potato. They simply registered their claim to some of the massive usage potatoes dominated.

Just as new products need to define their positioning clearly, there is often a need to reconsider and redefine. Established products and services are constantly trying to change the way in which they are seen.

Current advertising for All-Bran, a product that has been on the market since 1922, is seeking to change that product from its laxative connotation to that of a product that gives one the fibre a healthy diet needs. Dettol, a product that built up a strong position as a personal antiseptic, found that this high quality image was also a limitation since household disinfectant uses – cleaning lavatories, waste bins and so on – actually consumed much more product. These uses are dominated by low price, often private label disinfectants and the problem was how to acquire a proportion of the disinfectant volume without losing the high quality image that goes with personal antisepsis and which is the justification for Dettol's much higher price.

Always in these cases where repositioning is necessary, the rule is to make use of as much of the brand's ideological luggage as possible, to make the change as *unsurprising* as you can. Positions, it cannot be stressed enough, are long-term factors in the consumer's mind. Because there are so many products and services about, the consumer does not have the leisure or inclination to update his perception of a brand all that often so the perception always tends to lag behind the reality. The more modest the degree of change you require, the less likely you are to be disappointed.

CHAPTER 4

The Product Positioning and the Consumer Positioning

Look at the four ads pictured in Figure 3.

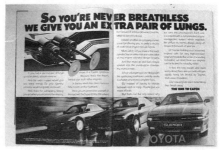

Figure 3 Product positioning concepts

Now compare them with the four ads in Figure 4.

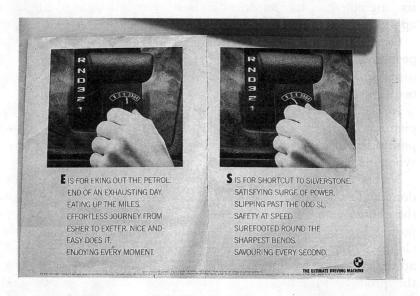

Figure 4   Consumer positioning concepts

What's the difference? Disregard the superficialities and look at these ads, please, not as advertisements but as positionings made flesh. They illustrate the two basic classifications of positioning. Those in Figure 3 are all what we call *product positionings*. Those in Figure 4 are what we call *consumer positionings*.

Product positioning concepts centre on the product or service. They position the product factually, in terms of what it will do, how it is made, its ingredients, its superiority over competition, its uses and applications.

Consumer positioning concepts on the other hand concentrate on the people who use the product or service. They position it in terms of its users, what sort of people they are, what kind of lifestyle they enjoy, the occasions the product fits into.

Notice that this is not simply a mechanical distinction – ads with big pictures of people are not automatically evidence of the consumer positioning any more than ads with big pictures of packs are necessarily synonymous with a product positioning.

Notice how in the product positioning ads while product shots are dominant, it's perfectly possible to illustrate the archetypal consumer, the child become book-consumer in the ad for book tokens. But the positioning is clear and product-oriented – books open new worlds to children. All these four examples position the product in terms of its advantages and characteristics – in the case of Ever Ready, spelling out the product advantages of a rechargeable battery; in the case of Amstrad, hitting the price argument which is the key plank of their positioning with characteristic directness; in the case of Toyota, explaining the innovation of twin valves per cylinder in a clever human parallel.

Conversely, let us look at the ads we have picked out as typifying consumer positioning concepts. Here the product is positioned in terms of its consumers.It is not important whether Dry Sack is dry or wet – the most important thing is to show that it is drunk by 'people like you'. Omega is quite open about the dream-fulfilment it offers – a watch which, believe it or not, is a ticket of admission to a particular type of society. Cardhu could trick you into thinking it's a product positioning story with its big bottle dominating the ad. But actually it's saying that people drink this malt whisky after dinner – which is a way of saying that it is consumed in a leisurely and discerning way, and on its own like a fine brandy, not mixed with ice and soda. And BMW? We have deliberately picked an ad which concentrates not merely on the product but on a comparatively small, technical feature, the two settings possible for the automatic transmission. Does it sell this feature technically? No, it explains it in terms of the lifestyle of the BMW driver: that sporty, well-off, youthful, skilful, committed driver who is the ideal of every BMW ad and of every BMW purchaser. A classic example of positioning a product in terms of its typical consumer.

23

What sort of conditions decide whether one uses the product positioning concept or the consumer positioning concept?

Product positioning concepts tend to be used for products of a functional, practical nature where actual product performance is important to the buying decision.

Consumer positioning concepts tend to be used for products which have a fashionable, image component and which ask the consumer to identify with them. Such products define lifestyles – cars are one example, clothing another, drinks and cigarette brands another.

Product positioning concepts tend to be used for products which have a genuine and significant product advantage – in ingredients, performance, packaging.

Consumer positioning concepts tend to be used for products which are imitative and familiar and whose technology has no novelty elements.

Let us now try to see which types of product concretely use which type of positioning concept and why.

Manufacturers define products by their ingredients – paper products, natural or man-made fibres, inorganic chemicals and so on.

Companies that are closer to the consumer classify products by the use the consumer puts them to – food, transport, entertainment, cleaning, medicines.

However, the most useful definition if we are trying to understand the consumer's way of seeing a product and selecting it, is *to classify products and services by the way that selection takes place*. Using this system I believe just about all consumer products and services can be broken down into the following five categories.

Functional products of daily use. These are the hosts of items we buy at the supermarket – detergents, lavatory cleaners, toothpaste, tea, tinned soup, breakfast cereals – to a startlingly large degree this group comprises some of the best known brands in the country.

Impulse items. These are much like the first group, low in cost, frequent in use – the distinction is that we buy them not as a daily necessity but as a little treat – soft drinks and sweets fall in this group as do minor items of clothing and magazines and some gifts.

High-ticket items. These are the things that we buy infrequently because they are expensive and last a long time. A house is for most families the highest-ticket item of all, but a car, washing machine, major pieces of furniture are in the same category – as, interestingly enough are some high-ticket, rarely used services like funerals, wedding receptions and so on.

Products of conspicuous consumption. These are the things we demonstrate our personality with, which we use to document what kind of people we are. The important factor is that people can see the brand and know how much it costs and what it signifies. Clothing is in this category and cars, though they are undoubtedly high-ticket items and have some of their characteristics, are the most effective social symbols of all. Many alcoholic drinks are in this area as are cigarettes, jewellery, the use of certain restaurants and even certain books.

Services. The distinctive characteristic of this area is the element of personal service. The person providing the service often *is* the service in the eyes of the customer.

The field is very large and diverse. It covers, for instance, the whole area of retailing, such traditional service businesses as pubs, restaurants and hairdressers, travel and holiday firms but also professional services such as those provided by solicitors and architects and the vast and very rapidly growing financial area. Because the product is often very diverse and more or less intangible, the field is a particularly complex one.

These varying categories of products and services all have their own rules in the game of positioning. In our next chapters we shall see what they are.

CHAPTER 5

Positioning a Functional Product

As we pointed out in our last chapter, the vast group of functional, daily use products provide us with many of our best-known brand names. They were the first type of product to be branded and the companies that own these brands are our most skilful marketers. They are also some of our largest and most consistent advertisers, investing millions in their brands over the years.

These facts have their consequences.

The markets in which such products live are oligopolies – there are a few large companies dominating the market. In breakfast cereals it is Kelloggs, Weetabix and Quaker. In detergents it is Procter & Gamble and Unilever. In coffee, Nestlé and General Foods.

The companies concerned know their markets well. They have worked in them for many years and they have developed all the product improvements that the consumers have come to expect. They also compete furiously, because these markets are mostly fairly mature – they are not expanding rapidly, if indeed at all. Add to that the dependence on the supermarkets (there are today just six very powerful and demanding retail groups that control 80 per cent of British grocery sales – another oligopoly) and the possibilities for profit growth in these markets is slim indeed. The only hope is to knock half a Nielsen point off one's competitor (see Glossary, p. 231), all the while knowing that that is his sole aim too.

This competitive situation means that although the firms concerned have a very thorough knowledge of their markets, they are very wary of letting any of it ever be published. There is a great deal of knowledge about such markets, but almost none of it is in the public domain.

This obliges us, if we are to be able to describe the mechanics of these markets in any useful way, to invent our own facts. Therefore, please take note, the statistics that follow are simple invention. Only by this expedient can we give a true impression of the way the markets for simple functional products work.

Let us imagine that you are a manufacturer of toilet soap. Let us further imagine that it is 1930 or thereabouts and that by buying up other companies, you and four other major manufacturers now dominate the soap market and each of you are looking for ways to increase your share. At this stage, one competitor (let us assume it is you) takes that new-fangled instrument research and sets out to find out what sort of qualities consumers want in toilet soaps.

(This is a totally new tack. Previously you assumed you knew what the consumers wanted, and your competitors did likewise. You were not wrong – you would not have achieved survival in this select oligopoly if your product had been wrong – but perhaps the researchers asking the consumer questions can show you something new.)

The research comes in and it shows:

a.   The consumers evaluate soap on five different dimensions:
    i.   Perceived mildness and gentleness to the skin.
    ii.   The 'purity' of ingredients.
    iii.   The ability of the soap to wash clean and remove odour.
    iv.   The availability of different colours.
    v.   The softness and fullness of the lather.

b.   These qualities are not all desired equally, though considerable overlaps exist. When consumers are asked to rank the particular qualities
    37 per cent put mildness to skin first
    22 per cent put purity of ingredients first
    16 per cent put cleaning and deodorancy first
    15 per cent put softness and fullness of lather first (but this was limited to hard water areas)
    10 per cent put availability of colours first.

c.   Asked to ascribe these qualities to particular brands, you are pleased to see that your brand comes out strongest in the two top areas of 'mildness to skin' and 'purity' and is in the middle of the field on all other dimensions.

With this piece of research available to you, what do you do?

I think it is quite clear what you do. You have a strong brand that appears to occupy the best position in the market. Since your brand is perceived as being mild and gentle to skin, and this appears to be the quality most wanted by the consumers, you launch as powerful an advertising campaign as you can muster stressing this attribute of your product. If all other things are equal you should see your brand grow rapidly – you are reminding the consumers of a characteristic that they want more than any other and which they already ascribe to your brand, so they are predisposed to believe it.

What then do your competitors do?

Probably the first thing they do is some research of their own. Not suprisingly it comes to much the same conclusions – it identifies more or less the same key dimensions, it shows the brands holding much the same positions that they held (with the exception that the mildness dimension is now more than ever a property of your brand since you have advertised it strongly for some years).

Inevitably one or two of your competitors will start advertising their brands for mildness to skin too. This would not worry you very much since the attribute was one that you have been able to make your own, but obviously you would be worried if any of their advertising campaigns seemed to communicate the idea of mildness better than yours did.

You would be more worried, I think, if one of them did what would probably be their next move and introduced a new brand designed specifically to attack the 'mildness to skin' segment. Such a brand would have a name that communicated mildness, would be the most mild product they could produce and would also perhaps boast an ingredient like cold cream to support its mildness claim.

Your reaction to this would be to introduce a new version of your product with cold cream in it too. You might introduce such a product beside your usual product or you might take the plunge and scrap the original product and go all over to the cold cream product. (On balance, as a wise marketer with a strong market leading product, I think you will do the first. After all, you do not know how the consumer will take to the cold cream idea. If it proves to be a wash-out then your cold cream version can be given a seemly but discreet burial while your original product continues to reign supreme.)

Meanwhile, other competitors will be doing other things. While the whole market is looking bewitched at mildness to skin and all brands are claiming this property with more or less success, one competitor will eventually say, 'The mildness to skin segment is the biggest – but it's only about 40 per cent at most. And there are six brands all claiming it. However, we have a brand that scores tops on deodorancy and that's something nobody talks about, even though 16 per cent of people want it. Let's go for that.'

They do. And they build a powerful Number Two brand on a deodorant claim, which in turn inspires its own crop of imitators.

Somebody will then try the same thing with lather, trying to make a regional brand in hard water areas – but perhaps they find the segment too small for profitable business and withdraw the product.

Meanwhile, your brand goes on holding on to its leadership and its long-term mildness position. Let us hope you invest in it wisely, doing everything to make sure it is at all times, if not the mildest soap on the market, at least the equal of any other brand in this dimension, and using the proceeds of market leadership to advertise strongly and identify your brand with mildness, building up a position that looks more and more impregnable.

If you do this, are you indeed impregnable?

Brands that have behaved like this do tend to be very hard to beat and to have a remarkable longevity. But obviously in this fast-changing world of ours no brand has a right to eternal life. You may find that, for instance, as more and more cosmetics are being used to care for skin, the mildness dimension slowly falls in importance (taking your brand, which is totally identified with it, into a lesser position). A new brand with a technological breakthrough that you cannot match may pre-empt the mildness position. Another brand may find a way of telling a mildness story which is more relevant to today's consumers than your way.

So what have we learnt from this little fable? What are the rules about product positioning in the area of functional, branded products?

1. *Product performance is key.* People accept that there are only marginal differences between products in this field. But they are strongly aware of these marginal differences. If the product is not up to the mark it cannot survive.

2. *Product positioning concepts are the rule.* This flows directly from the central importance of product performance. Also these low-cost, workaday, often-bought products have no particular glamour or prestige: they are consumed at home and we have little idea which brands our friends and our role-models buy.

3. *There are key dimensions that segment the market.* Different consumers look for different performance strengths and give their allegiance to the brands that seem to be strongest in the relevant performance areas.

4. *The market leader tends to have the strongest position on the key dimension.* Brands that achieve long-term leadership of their market tend to be

those that have made the key performance dimension desired by consumers their own.

5. *The number two brand tends to have the strongest position on the second most desired performance dimension.* This assertion is not susceptible of proof, since there are so many markets where the performance dimensions are uncharted and brand performance is diffuse, but there are certainly many cases where it is true. It is also at least logical that you can be a powerful challenger by being utterly different to number one and standing for everything that number one is weak in, rather than being a pallid, me-too imitation of number one.

6. *Positions, once occupied, can be enduring.* We buy products of this kind so often that their purchase becomes routine. Life is too short to examine all the options every time we need a kitchen cleaner. Once we identify a particular product as being the best in the dimension which is most important to us, we are likely to continue buying it. The market leader will usually only be unseated by allowing his product to be overtaken or by a quite unprecedentedly better advertising campaign (in most cases it takes *both* of these and also demands that the leader be inattentive and stupid).

For the person who is aiming to position a product in this broad category of functional, workaday, practical products, there are three fundamental rules to be followed:

- Learn which are the key dimensions of performance in the consumer's mind
- Attempt to achieve product superiority on the key dimension, or, failing that, on the next most important dimension
- Be totally single-minded in communicating this positioning of your product.

CHAPTER 6

Positioning the Impulse Product

As we have already noted, the impulse product is very like the classic branded product. Like the functional branded product, it is bought frequently and brand choice is often more or less a matter of habit; not much consideration goes into the matter at all.

Impulse products are like that only more so. They are bought just because we happen to feel like a little treat, because the product takes our fancy. The corollary is that these products are very dependent on achieving wide distribution. If they are not seen, they are not bought. Coca-Cola has always expressed it as being 'within an arm's length of desire'.

Such products are necessarily very large and consistent advertisers. Particularly, they spend a great deal on establishing a presence at the point of sale with permanent signs, showcards and anything else that can convey a name and perhaps a simple slogan. Products in the impulse category depend on the unthinking, conditioned reflex – see them and buy them.

There is no other category where awareness translates so perfectly into sales. Impulse products look for maximum awareness of:

1. The brand name.
2. The package.
3. An extremely simple advertising message, preferably with some inherent memorability.

The first two are obvious requirements. Perhaps we should spend a little time on the third and understand why impulse products need this sort of advertising.

They are, first, products that cost little and occupy little of our time. So consequently we are prepared to expend very little intellectual effort upon them. The question of whether Coke tastes better than Pepsi is a question that exercises the two companies but is of total insignificance to the people who drink one or the other. It is therefore very hard to give people logical, factual reasons why they should prefer one product to another and have these reasons believed or even listened to.

Also, unlike those products of conspicuous consumption that we shall be considering soon, these simple impulse products confer no distinction on their users. Cigarettes and beer have much in common with them, but they also have an extra dimension that distinguishes them. Cigarettes and beer define the type of person you are and the personality you want to present to the world. Simple impulse products do this to no significant degree, they are usually so universal that their archetypal consumer can be just anybody at all.

So such products use product positioning concepts or consumer positioning concepts indifferently. The common factor is that any positioning is always extremely simple. Coca-Cola positions itself with magnificent simplicity as 'the real thing' – a product positioning that suggests that simply because it is everywhere and is known to everybody and drunk by everybody it is *right* and all others are somehow pallid imitations.

Pepsi talks about 'the Pepsi generation' and tries to deal with the omnipresence of Coke by stressing its suitability for that (admittedly vast and amorphous) group that comprises the major users of soft drinks.

The dominance of Coke and Pepsi in the USA (which accounts for more than half the world's consumption of soft drinks and in which market these two brands hold some 60 per cent) means that all other brands have the problem of overcoming the conditioned reflex that leads to Coke or Pepsi before they even begin to sell their own brand. You usually don't even think of Dr Pepper or 7-Up until you are halfway through your Coke.

7-Up had a campaign that tackled this perennial problem when they positioned their lemonade as 'the Uncola'. This might seem to be defeatist and negative. In fact, it leads the consumer to remember your product even if his conditioned thinking is skewed totally towards Colas. It actually gets 7-Up considered in that field. And should you have the feeling, 'I'd like something different from a Cola today', then the choice of 7-Up is pre-programmed.

Notice that this positioning could only work in the field of impulse products. For any item which is the subject of serious consideration and significant expenditure, for any product which is expected to provide a

Figure 5 The Uncola – how 7-Up positioned itself against Coke and Pepsi

measurable performance, the positioning as 'not the same as the market leader' is woefully inadequate. But in the field of impulse products its simplicity and memorability enables it to break through to your consciousness and perhaps even overcome your conditioned behaviour.

Some branded products that do not really belong in the impulse product category tend to use the same mechanics in their marketing. In fact, these mechanics are the oldest form of brand marketing. In the nineteenth-century world of the first branded goods, establishing pack identity and a simple slogan was the accepted way of advertising. Beechams Pills were lauded as 'worth a guinea a box', Bisto simply had the one word 'Ah!' before it. The popular PG Chimps carry the technique on to television and into the present day. It is significant that the product claim in these noticeable but fairly meaningless commercials is the bland 'Tea you can really taste'. Tea brands, biscuits, salt, flour – simple products that verge on commodities – all tend to use the simple techniques of impulse products like sweets, chewing gum, soft drinks.

Meanwhile some impulse products attempt – often very successfully – to go in the other direction. Many of the most successful big-selling brands of confectionery in this country (where incidentally the per capita consumption of sweets is the highest in the world) deliberately seek a positioning that has more substance than most impulse products.

The most successful brands position themselves not as 'candy bars', to use an Americanism, but as food. Kit-Kat is a legitimate snack at work or in a packed lunch. Mars is something that gives you energy in your work and leisure. Other brands like Fudge and Milky Way stress that they are modest in size and not filling. This sort of positioning takes the curse of self-indulgence off what are in themselves self-indulgent products. They are vital rationalisations to enable the censorious Protestant conscience to be stilled and sweets to be enjoyed.

CHAPTER 7

Positioning the High-Ticket Item

Expensive, infrequently-purchased items have their own special problems in positioning.

Essentially these stem from the fact that people only consider these products at all at the time when they are thinking of entering the market. It works like this: a couple will decide that it is time to buy a washing machine. For some six months they will look at ads for washing machines with greater interest than they have shown before. They will slowly build up a reasonable awareness of what the market has to offer (by no means a complete one, incidentally, it will probably be limited to a few makes that they have decided to look into further). They will then procure brochures from these makes and, on studying these brochures, and also based on visits to shops, they will finally come to a firm decision. The chosen machine will be purchased and installed. It will be the subject of some months of heightened interest to confirm that the choice was indeed a good one (and during this time the advertisements will still be devoured with great avidity) but fairly soon it will settle down to become an unremarked piece of the furnishings and will continue so until it either needs replacement or growing prosperity makes it possible and desirable to replace it. Such, in essence, is the manner in which all such items are bought.

Two exceptions are the two highest-ticket items that most people ever buy – a car and a house. These purchases are so important that they virtually never fade away into that limbo that less exciting items occupy when their purchase is not imminent. This is evinced in the fact that there is a very active branch of journalism that simply informs people about the latest cars, while living styles and interior decoration also have their own, keenly-supported media. There are not many commercial products that are the subject of such unremitting interest.

The great deal of interest displayed in houses and cars comes about because these are clearly products of conspicuous consumption as well as being major occasional expenses. What you drive and where you live are vital statistics that say a lot about you. Correspondingly, there is a lot of role-playing in connection with cars and houses. Drivers with modest incomes are keenly aware of the technical details of the latest Porsche or Aston Martin. Dwellers in simple semi-detached houses read with great interest about the lifestyles played out in significantly grander surroundings.

So while cars and houses also obey some of the rules that we shall adduce for high-ticket items they are not subject to them all, simply because of the much greater intensity of interest they arouse. What is much more typical for high ticket items is a generally low level of interest that only rises (but then dramatically) when a purchase is about to take place.

A further characteristic of these products is that they often tend or tended to have a boom period when the household establishment grew by leaps and bounds till it reached a saturation level after which the replacement volume became the annual market size. We have seen this many times. The rapid growth in TV set establishment at the imminent arrival of ITV, followed by later spurts of demand with the establishment of further programmes; the washing machine boom between 1955 and 1965; the present rapid growth in double glazing and in videorecorders.

Brands become established in the boom periods when the market is enjoying such large volume sales that heavy advertising is possible and, because very large numbers of people are actively thinking of purchase, consumer awareness of advertising is high. This vestigial awareness carries over into the quieter periods when sales are lower. The first consequence is that a manufacturer who has not established his name in the boom time will find it quite hard to get known afterwards.

It is also noticeable that, except when a purchase is actively being considered, most consumers are unaware of specific advantages and technical features offered by individual manufacturers. In fact, they cannot be interested in such features unless they are quite earth-shaking, which, in the nature of things, they rarely are. However, once an imminent purchase has been decided upon, all this changes and the willingness to compare details of technology increases dramatically.

The consequence is that the brands that people take into the charmed circle of 'ones they are going to look at more closely' are chosen largely on superficial generalised impressions that may well be severely out of date. Yet unless a brand gets taken into this group it will probably never come to the detailed assessment that precedes actual purchase.

The whole matter puts the industry in a severe quandary. Should it advertise every minor and major improvement and accept that this advertising will only have any effect (and even find any interest) among the small group who are actively looking at this time? Or should it attempt to position all the products of the company in a generalised and positive direction, relying on brochures to do the detailed selling of features and models?

Experience suggests that the latter is the more effective strategy. It is the strategy employed by Maytag for many years in the US, positioning all its products on a clear and consistent line of reliability and long service. It has similarly been the strategy employed by Zanussi in the UK, stressing modernity and high technology in TV advertising for a name that was virtually unknown before. Leaving the selling of individual models to brochures and in-store material has a further financial justification – necessarily lengthy information can more readily be accommodated in media where every word is not at a premium.

Things are different, however, in boom times. Then – for instance in the washing machine growth of the 1950s – a very large percentage of the readers of popular magazines and the viewers of TV were actively in the market. As that period showed, detailed product-oriented advertising paid off handsomely.

Summing up the positioning of high-ticket items, we can say:

1. Determine what percentage of the media public are in fact in the market, i.e. what is the cycle of replacement or the incidence of first acquisition, measured against the total population?

2. If it is high – arbitrarily we could say if the rate of replacement is 25 per cent or over per year, or if one household in four or more expressed the intention of buying in the current year – then use clear product positioning advertising that stresses the technical benefits of your product.

3. If the purchase rate is well below this, then use company positioning concepts that stress the overall qualities of all your company's products and do this in a consumer-relevant way.

4. Ascertain whether your high-ticket item has any element of personal prestige or lifestyle identification. If it has, do not fail to exploit this motivation, too.

Positioning Products of Conspicuous Consumption

Products of conspicuous consumption are things you wear, smoke, drink, drive – even visit. The most important thing about them is that other people know you use them. They are part of the personality you project to the world.

The actual phrase, if I remember correctly, was coined by Thorstein Veblen who observed that the best way to document wealth was by having two footmen standing on the back of your carriage. Foot*men*, because male servants were known to be more expensive than female. Two, because obviously two were more expensive than one. Standing on the back of your carriage, because there they were seen to be doing nothing useful at all.

Now, most of the products that carry out this function for us today are not so totally useless and obviously ostentatious as that. They have a valid functional use. And they are mostly quite modest little luxuries. But that their real importance for the consumer is the demonstration of personality cannot be denied. This is often the real reason why you buy the product at all. And it is almost always the reason why you choose that particular type, that particular brand.

Clothing is a classic example – and has been ever since there were sumptuary laws that forbade an aspiring bourgeoisie to dress in the fabrics and styles reserved for the nobility. Today, the clothes you wear define you as a City Gent, as a countrified traditionalist, as a modern swinger, as a bejeaned egalitarian.

Cars are a similar example. The function of the car is transport and convenience. But, this basic function apart, every further decision the car-buyer makes is a compromise between the aspirations he wishes to

Figure 6 Clothing is the conspicuous consumption product *par excellence*

document and the resources of his cheque book.

Cigarettes are another case in point. The real function of a cigarette is to serve a minor addiction and provide some sort of relaxation and relief from tension. Yet, who can doubt that these functions are totally secondary to the help a cigarette gives in providing a prop to confidence, in punctuating speech, in wearing the pack as a kind of badge?

In those countries where there is a State monopoly on tobacco, it is commonplace that the workman smokes the monopoly brand (which is usually cheaper) all week and at home. But on the weekend he puts on his best suit, sits at a pavement cafe – and negligently tosses a packet of Marlboro or Benson & Hedges in front of him.

It is important to realise that products that are props in role playing are not only used to demonstrate social status, or wealth, or youth. There are all sorts of personality shadings, allegiances, enthusiasms and convictions that can be discreetly but effectively communicated to the world by the choice and conspicuous use of a product.

Why is it that middle-class intellectuals tend to smoke cigarettes that were old-fashioned working-class brands 20 years ago? Why is it that real ale is not popular in the spit and sawdust of the public bar but in the plush fleshpots of the saloon? (Or perhaps more precisely among people

Figure 7 VW in the US – a protest against Detroit

who would have been patrons of one or other of those convenient class-oriented divisions if they still existed in our pubs.) Find a true working-class pub and you will usually find a stronghold of keg bitter.

And just as there are people who use their choice of car to demonstrate their technical knowledge, their driving skill and their youthful, playboy personality, there are people who use their choice of car to say, 'I think that's all a bit childish. I want sensible, basic transport. An honest reliable car. I'm not a sucker to the wiles of Detroit.'

> Documenting this last personality by driving a Volkswagen was a very popular activity for middle-class, East Coast Americans in the 1960s and it made Volkswagen the runaway success of the car market. The point is, however, that this is just as much a consciously cultivated personality as the playboy type it affects to smile at.
>
> Interestingly enough, the Volkswagen never had this sort of image in Germany. There it really was the basic product that motorised a whole class of people who could never have afforded any other car. In Germany the car that demonstrated that you were not one to succumb to the manipulation of the motor industry, that you were not a slave to speed and horsepower, that you had a relaxed Gallic (and, by definition, very non-German) chic, was the Citroen 2CV. In provincial France, where the 2CV was simply basic transport for peasant farmers, it had, of course, no chic at all.

In products of conspicuous consumption, the intention of documenting personality, of demonstrating what sort of person one is, is a major component in the buying decision. So naturally consumer positioning concepts are used to advertise them. After all, the lifestyle is 90 per cent of what the consumer buys.

However, this does not have to mean that such campaigns should neglect the product or that their ads should be low on product information.

Cars are also high-ticket items. They are complex pieces of technology with a host of technical features. Understandably, car advertising tends to give full treatment to all the technical advantages. This is legitimate in a product about which there is much to say. It also has, in conspicuous consumption products, another and equally vital function – it enables the purchaser to justify his choice.

It is known that car purchasers read car advertisements particularly intently just *after* they have bought a new car – they are mugging up what to tell their friends.

Product information in conspicuous consumption products advertising has another important function – it consciously builds what I can only call the *mythology* of the product.

It is in fact very typical of successful conspicuous consumption products that they have their own mythology – like the Dunhill white spot, like the RR nameplate of Rolls Royce that used to be red but became irrevocably black on the death of Henry Royce in 1933. Successful advertising for such products builds this mythic quality. It is, for instance, not unusual to find lengthy product copy in ads for wines, whisky, brandy and so on. Read it carefully and you will realise it is not giving you hard product facts on which to base a logical judgement, it is skilfully weaving a cloak of romance and legend around the product. And at the same time it is giving you useful titbits of information to fascinate or bore your friends with.

The successful campaigns for such products are particularly strong in this mythic element, building a special world round the product. Burberry does it well and with superb economy. Marlboro has become the world's most successful cigarette with an exciting, masculine, cowboy world that has been just as effective in the Far East as the Far West and almost everywhere in between. And what Guinness has never been able to recapture fully since deserting its familiar slogans and its

Figure 8   Marlboro – a position that works for for the brand worldwide

zoo keepers and its strange menagerie and a whole fascinating, enjoyable, very English world reminiscent of Lewis Carroll, has been this mythic quality. Faced with the problem of a dark, heavy, out-of-fashion beer, they have tried to sell the beer as beer and forgotten the mythology. Sales have gone obstinately down year after year.

Because of this mythological element, products of conspicuous consumption cannot readily be repositioned. One can, at best, try to give a position that has become outdated a subtle shift into today's world. One can try to stress the positives of a position and a personality that is already known and minimise some of the negatives. One cannot really alter it.

All the evidence is that if you wish to take advantage of a new trend in one of the conspicuous consumption markets, you are better advised to introduce a new product than attempt to reposition an established one.

The brands to profit from the trend towards lighter Scotch were unfamiliar brands, J&B Rare and Cutty Sark. The attempt to introduce a light VAT 69 was a failure.

There has been a tremendous shift in cigarette brands lately and the brands to profit have been the new ones. None of the attempts to revive major brands of the past – Players, Capstan, Gold Flake, Senior Service, Churchman's, to name just a few – have worked.

Brands of detergents and foods can much more easily be changed and repositioned and line extensions can much more easily be added. Why does it not work in conspicuous consumption products?

Probably because these products have their entire *raison d'etre* in the personality they project. They are simply compromised and unbelievable if they make a jump that is too large – like a leading Conservative suddenly switching his allegiance to Labour. Functional products are simply products – conspicuous consumption products are, by contrast, almost *people*.

This is probably the reason why such products are not readily amenable to advertising approaches that seek to beat prejudice in factual argument. One cannot be detached and simply look at the facts. The loyalty to a car, a cigarette brand, a perfume, is instinctive and total, reminiscent of the loyalty expected to one's country. To evaluate, to argue, to look at both sides is a kind of treachery and one compromises oneself if one does so.

A filter cigarette was introduced by Churchman's in the 1950s under the name Churchman's Tipped. The advertising showed smokers tasting the Churchman's Tipped and a traditional non-tipped cigarette under blind test conditions and choosing the Churchman's Tipped for its taste:

a campaign that was more typical of detergent advertising than the cigarette advertising of the day. Even though the trend towards tipped cigarettes was very strong, Churchman's Tipped failed to make any impression on the market.

Because of the great commitment that one feels towards a brand in this field, shifts – when they do occur – are slow and discreet. There is a long period of flirtation with the new brand before change takes place. But if the new brand is able to increase the frequency of its purchase during this period then it may ultimately take over. The whole process is like a divorce and remarriage.

Products of conspicuous consumption (and the many products that have a significant element of this type of motivation in their buying behaviour) need especially sensitive handling. The main rules can be summed up as follows:

1. *Understand the mechanics and parameters of the market.* These are rarely as simple as young/old, upmarket/downmarket, conservative/ progressive. It is generally a multi-dimensional model with some positions in decline and others in the ascendant.

2. *Understand the position the product occupies and do not attempt to change it radically.*

3. *Do everything possible to strengthen your product's inherent imagery and 'mythology'.*

4. *Aim for long-term consistency rather than short-term shifts and tactical gains.*

CHAPTER 9

Positioning a Service

In our list of basic product types in Chapter Four we included retail and other services and financial services. We can consider these together from the point of view of positioning since they have the same fundamental differences that separate them from products of the branded goods type.

These are:

1. *Services are non-standardised.* Whereas branded goods can be branded not least because they are identical – one tin of Heinz baked beans is just the same as another – even the simplest services are not standard. Every haircut from the same barber differs. Each piece of legal advice from a solicitor is tailor-made to a particular situation. Even in those fields where service companies have attempted to offer standardised 'products' as they revealingly call them (for instance in the financial field, where a product can be a particular type of mortgage, a particular insurance policy and the like) these products have much greater individuality than the branded goods field would tolerate.

2. *There is usually direct contact between the person who provides the service and the customer.* Many services are one-to-one in the way the solicitor or the barber are. In smaller shops you buy direct from the proprietor and seek his or her advice and even in larger shops you treat the sales assistant as a representative of the organisation. Even someone who is clearly in a dealer's position (such as a travel agent selling a package tour) is still treated as a source of advice and counsel.

These two factors are of course the reasons why services are the home of the small company and the self-employed. One of the large company's inherent strengths is the rationalisations and cost-savings that come from producing a standardised product in massive quantities.

They have also tended to limit the importation of formal marketing techniques into the service field. This is not simply due to the size of companies involved. Many service companies (airlines, retail groups, insurance companies and building societies are obvious examples) are easily of a size to practise such techniques. It is due much more to an assumption that a constantly changing, intangible product was not susceptible to this type of selling and that the close contact the company enjoyed with the final customer made such techniques unnecessary. This is an attitude which is changing fast. Today such companies are often overtaking the branded goods companies in terms of advertising expenditure. For instance, the ten largest individual budgets in the UK in 1986 were:

Company	Budget (£000s)
Hygena/MFI	19,223
Dixons	13,452
Currys	13,319
MSC Action for Jobs	10,393
Benson & Hedges Special Filter	10,047
Electricity Council	9,428
Peugeot 309	9,315
Comet	8,970
Players Superking	8,886
Texas Home Care	8,850

Five retailers, one public utility and one public service campaign in the top ten! And, perhaps even more significant but ignored in these figures because it was clearly a one-off occurrence, a staggering 33 million for the British Gas share flotation.

This increase in advertising expenditure is usually the first step towards more sophisticated marketing and this is clearly the case with many services in Britain.

Examples of this are:

The growth of franchising. This makes it possible for a small business to 'clone' itself many times over without being dependent on cash it has itself generated and without needing massive resources of staff. There is no reason why this should be restricted to services but most of the successful franchises are services. Eating has been transformed by fast food franchisers such as Kentucky Fried Chicken and Wimpy. Macdonalds, until recently fighting shy of franchising in Britain, is now operating franchises here, a system on which its domination of the US market has been built.

The familiar 'tied house' system operated by the breweries is also in effect a kind of franchising, as is the system by which petrol filling stations are operated. While it can be claimed that the product sold here is clearly a traditional branded product – petrol or beer – there is also a sizeable element of service in the sale and this is provided by the outlet, which in turn is identified with the brewer or the oil company much more closely than is usual with retail outlets.

Other franchises are invading what are traditionally 'individual' services. Prontaprint competes with the small local printer, Dyno Rod with the independent plumber, Poppies with that sterling individualist the 'daily'.

The expansion of services into related fields. This is happening at a fast rate in one of the traditionally independent areas – estate agency. A few years ago there were 15,000 estate agents' offices owned by some 12,000 firms: ie the typical firm had 1.25 offices. Today Lloyds Bank owns some 200 estate agency offices, closely followed by the Prudential, and very many other financial institutions are looking at this market. The day when a few large financial companies own half the estate agents in Britain can easily be foreseen. That much the same thing will happen with opticians, given their impressive profit records and the growth that an ageing population will inevitably bring, can be regarded as certain.

Deliberately restricting the scope of a business to gain recognition and competence. This is the technique used by a number of very successful retailers who specialise in a limited range of goods with the aim of becoming *the* experts in that category. This is the secret behind the specialist exhaust replacement services as against general garages. In the fashion field there have been several examples recently, including Tie Rack, Knickerbox and The Sock Shop. The items sold must be fast-moving, there must be a need for a wide and differing range of styles, types or sizes and they must be items comparatively neglected by mainstream retailers. Significantly, such businesses are pre-destined users of franchising, since they require only a small investment, are very well-suited to owner operation, and a useful service can be provided by the franchiser in identifying suppliers and negotiating with them.

The use of marketing techniques to achieve growth in areas where they have not been used before. In a few short years after 1978, the American lawyer Joel Hyatt built his company into the largest law practice in the USA by advertising his law clinics on TV. So far British solicitors have made no significant use of their new freedom to advertise, but the days cannot be far distant ...

Given the different and changing nature of services, what then are the rules in positioning them?

First, of course, a classic product positioning is out of the question in most cases. Even a positioning that seeks to give the service a specialised competence in a particular area is dangerous unless the business actually does intend to specialise in that area.

Second, since the part played by staff in the sale is so large, staff are inevitably a major target audience of one's persuasive efforts. We have already mentioned Avis. Perhaps one of the most effective parts of this whole operation was that it required counter staff to wear a button proclaiming 'We try harder'. It is difficult to be unco-operative and discourteous while so identified.

In most service operations, staff – be they airline stewards, sales assistants, negotiators at estate agents, insurance salesmen, waiters, bank clerks – really *are* the company they work for. The product we get is often a rather intangible thing. Transport from A to B, petrol that vanishes into the tank without our even seeing it, a mortgage that is a piece of paper and a sizeable monthly cheque to be paid out. The only really tangible aspect of the company is this person who represents them.

Add to this the fact that a service company usually has a major investment and a major part of its cost in people and the need to reflect and include the people who offer that service in the positioning concept will be clear.

British Airways make heroes of their cabin staff in their TV advertising showing embarrassed business travellers in trouble being saved by a Superman-like steward or stewardess. It is done in a tongue-in-cheek way (and when we come to study the techniques of producing ads we will see that a modicum of humour is a way of presenting the unbelievable acceptably) but its message is clear. The first target for that message is not the traveller, not the travel agent, but the staff themselves.

It is a corollary of the subordinate nature of the product that services are especially likely to lay great emphasis on corporate identity. This simply means having a common design theme that goes through all stationery (about the only thing you get from professional and financial services are pieces of paper – it is obviously right to have those pieces of paper looking good), retail premises, livery of vehicles (especially

Figure 9 Advertising for services must involve staff – British Airways makes heroes of them

important for transport companies, this), uniforming of staff, advertising style elements and so on. One of the most popular and now most widely-used typefaces, Gill Sans, was in fact designed for London Transport in the 1930s as part of the comprehensive establishment of a design entity by Eric Gill.

Of all service companies, financial companies have the problem of intangibility of product to perhaps the most extreme extent. At the same time, their product is inextricably bound up with that most concrete of substances, money.

This leads to extreme dichotomies in positioning and advertising. On the one hand, it is necessary to stress marginal differences in financial terms since people want the best buy – and the differences between this building society account and that are generally marginal – and this requires a lot of wordy explanation which is often only partially understood and, to make matters worse, is subject to constant change. On the other hand, image components play a great part in the selection of financial institutions. You do not even consider a company unless you see it as honest and straight-dealing, quick to settle (if it is an insurance company), offering total safety for your savings (if it is a building society), helpful and 'on your side' (if it is a bank).

This leads to two aspects of the advertising for financial institutions: complex, hard-to-understand 'product' advertising that does precious little for the positioning of the institution, and very generalised and boring 'image' advertising that is often as unreadable as a company report and about as far from day-to-day reality.

In summary, then, can we produce a short list of 'do's' for the positioning of services?

Do attempt to reflect a consistent, attractive personality in all manifestations of the organisation that reach the public.

Do aim for a recognisable, human personality to compensate for an intangible or diverse product range.

Do incorporate your staff as a key target group in all your efforts and treat their motivation as a major objective.

Do use any techniques that may be unused or under-used in your field. Their impact is the greater because of their rarity.

Do stress any specialisation you have – it will help you resist the generalised, all-things-to-all-people image which is the bane of service companies.

CHAPTER 10

Positioning for Leaders and Challengers

We have already suggested in this book that the positioning needs of market leaders are somewhat different to those of products challenging that leadership. This is an important concept and needs to be analysed in a little more depth.

The characteristics of a market leader

First, perhaps we should understand the unique strengths and characteristics of a market leader. They are considerable.

The market leader has usually either founded the market, as Hoover did with the vacuum cleaner market or Nescafé did with instant coffee, or has taken over leadership so long ago that it has become totally identified with the market and the category. *This means the market leader is the brand everybody thinks of automatically when they think of this category.*

The market leader has, by definition, a larger income from its sales than any challenger, and this means the resources to advertise more heavily. Though challengers may raise the resources to outspend the market leader for a limited time, unless they build up comparable sales, they are hardly likely to persist in such a spendthrift activity. *Market leaders usually have heavier advertising.*

In addition, *the market leader often benefits from the advertising of challengers.* While this is not always the case, we know that a lot of advertising for other companies' breakfast cereals, for instance, is ascribed to Kelloggs by inattentive viewers.

The market leader enjoys the best distribution. This rule is virtually automatic. In the battle for supermarket distribution today, in which the supermarket's own brands have a very important role, it is often only the market leader that has an automatic place on the shelves apart from the own label product. Outlets where space is limited will always stock the market leader knowing that it is universally acceptable.

The market leader has established itself and its advertising over years. It has, presumably, a strong positioning otherwise it would not be in the position it enjoys. This strong positioning, reinforced by constant repetition in advertising, becomes the norm for the market. It becomes the issue that consumers think of first. *The market leader dictates the battlefield on which his challengers fight.*

With these impressive advantages, a well-entrenched market leader is very hard to attack. There may be cases where a challenger can actually take over leadership in the short term but these are rare. They usually come about because the market leader is fatally flawed in some way or makes a fundamental mistake. Even though a competitor may be able to muster more money, for the reasons we have listed above this often does not cut the ice it should. There are, of course, some situations in which a challenger can risk a frontal attack.

For instance, *the market leader may have failed to keep his product competitive.* A challenger has a better product and the market leader may not update his product to equal it. While product superiority is a Grail devoutly to be wished, the inertia of the market leader is such that he will not easily be displaced unless the superiority is sizeable, obvious and relevant to the consumer. And it is often fatally easy for the market leader to incorporate the same product improvement. With the funds at his disposal he will often do it nationally, while you are still playing around in a test market!

The market leader can be outspent consistently and over the long term. This usually only happens when a very big company gets into a market owned at the moment by minnows. (Don't count on the inequity continuing, however. Often a result of a challenge from a major company will be another major company taking over the market leader and continuing the battle with more equal resources.)

Successful challenges against market leaders can more readily be mounted using what Liddell-Hart calls the Indirect Approach. The aim here is to seek a way into the market which avoids challenging the market leader head on. For instance:

The market is changing. This may happen when the market leader is totally committed to one trade channel while overall market sales are moving to some other type of outlet and at a very fast pace. This can lead to the challenger establishing itself in this new trade channel and simply waiting for the trend of the market to make it number one.

The consumer is changing. A challenger can see that the complex of consumer habits and wishes that had given the market leader his leadership are ceasing to be dominant. A growing number of consumers are not ideally served by the market leader. A challenger can position himself specifically against the needs of this other consumer group.

The market leader does not serve a key consumer group adequately. Obviously, if this is the case, a valuable franchise can be built up by positioning a challenger specifically for this group. Provisos are that the market leader really doesn't serve them and that their numbers are large enough to build a market.

Positioning concepts for market leaders

Market leaders have a wide choice of possible positioning concepts but these all tend to have certain factors in common.

Market leaders seek to exclude nobody. Persil has held on to leadership of the UK detergent market (with some ups and downs) for 30 years. One of the keys to this has been a friendly, all-inclusive positioning of the product for 'Mums' which is acceptable to virtually all and alienates nobody. A market leader should aim to be an accepted favourite with everybody – and this includes being the *second* favourite brand with those people who do not choose it first.

Market leaders go for the heart of the market. Shaefer has become the number one Brewery in the East of the US, its positioning summed up in the slogan 'The one beer to have, when you're having more than one'. In many markets – beer is certainly one of them – there are heavy consumers and light consumers. It is usually wise for a market leader to consolidate its position with the heavy users.

Market leaders seek to widen the market. Johnson Wax has always rigorously avoided any advertising claim for any of the company's polishes that suggests polishing can be reduced. They are aware that polishing as a habit is declining anyway and they have a heavy investment in the market. They do not believe in promoting reduced polishing even for a temporary advantage. Campbell's Soup, the overwhelming market leader in the US, has always used its advertising to promote soup-eating, knowing it will profit more from an increase in the total market than it can ever take off other brands.

Positioning concepts for challengers

Unlike market-leading brands, challenging brands have to position themselves in a totally different way.

Challengers need a sharp thrust. Whereas a market leader can be easy-going and friendly to everybody, a challenger needs to identify its prospective buyers clearly and convince them powerfully and incontrovertibly of its superiority. Amstrad's chosen position is as a low price manufacturer whose products claim to do everything the more expensive competitors can do. They communicate it very aggressively and outspokenly.

Challengers are merciless to the weaknesses of the leader. If the market leader has a weakness (and if the challenger is strong enough for a head-to-head fight) the challenger can accentuate this weakness and make the leader's customers more aware of it. Procter & Gamble's Scope mouthwash has done this by talking about the leader in the market, Listerine, giving 'medicine breath'. Tylenol, Johnson & Johnson's pain reliever, did the same thing against aspirin-based products that had dominated the market for years by branding such products as likely to cause stomach upset.

Figure 10   P&G's Scope attacking a brand leader at its point of weakness

Figure 11 Charlie – a challenger that became a leader

Challengers need to identify their own consumers and alienate them from the market leader. Just as the market leader operates a broad church aiming to be everybody's best (or at the very least second best) friend, a challenger needs to secure his customers by suggesting to them how the leader has failed to serve them or understand them. Perfumes, since time immemorial have been positioned as exaggeratedly feminine, sultry, romantic, luxurious. Revlon's Charlie did away with all that, typifying its ideal user as a trouser-suited working girl – so much so that it became market leader.

All these comments on leader and challenger apply just as much when the challenger comes from the same firm as the leader. One of the most important characteristics of modern marketing is that marketers have come to realise that products occupy positions that are not readily changed and therefore are increasingly ready to give a new market segment its own new brand.

At the same time, however, they are often alarmed at the prospect of spending millions on a new challenger simply to chip away at their own market leading brand.

There is no easy answer here, but it has to be said that if you can do it,

55

so can somebody else. Somebody else has the enormous stimulus that they do not have any investment in the market as it is. If you can see a way – technological, through trading practices or by positioning – to unseat your most successful product, rest assured your competitors can see it too.

> In 1960, Gillette seemed invincible in the shaving market, with over 75 per cent of the total UK blade market. In that year Wilkinson introduced the first stainless steel blade and in two years had taken 15 per cent market share. In the US market, where Gillette was equally dominant, Wilkinson was also as successful as its limited production would allow and the example of the UK market had alerted Schick-Eversharp and Philip Morris's Personna to the possibilities of this product. Yet it was the Autumn of 1963 before Gillette brought out its own stainless steel blade and, though Gillette was able to bounce back, the experience had cost the company a lot of money and a lot of its self-respect.
>
> Why the delay? Only a few years before Gillette had scored a tremendous success with its Super Blue blade, its first new product for years and a massively profitable item. Even though the stainless steel blade could be sold at a significantly higher price, it gave the shaver more shaves and, depending on how this equation worked out, there was a very real possibility that both volume and profit would be negatively affected. Gillette simply could not face the fact that the Super Blue product had become outdated only a couple of years after its spectacularly successful launch.

The moral is simple. If there is a possible way your market leader can be attacked, you are wise to do the attacking yourself. You may well end up with a market that is smaller, less profitable, tougher all round. But if the possibility for attack exists then you are still better advised to take it than to leave it to a competitor. If he does it you may be left with nothing at all.

CHAPTER 11

The Business of Business-to-Business

There is a large and growing volume of advertising that now dignifies itself with the title 'business-to-business'. It is advertising for goods or services that are sold to traders or to corporate or institutional customers. It looks like a brand new category of advertising (and is being energetically promoted as a new discipline with its own rules and principles). Yet when you look at it closely it seems to be very like that familiar animal that was usually abbreviated to 'trade & tech'.

It is certainly true that business is a massive customer for all sorts of goods and services. It is also fairly clear that a business does not buy in exactly the same way as an individual. But I find it very hard to accept that this is a separate category with rules of its own.

There are two reasons for this.

First, there are very large numbers of products that simply cannot be fitted exclusively into the consumer or into the 'business' or 'industrial' category. You think of passenger cars as consumer goods – but 75 per cent of new cars are bought by companies. There is a vast growth market in building materials sold through the DIY chains – and the smaller jobbing builder is one of their major customers. The major utilities like British Telecom, British Gas, the CEGB sell to both markets. The airlines depend on the business customer for the overwhelming percentage of their full-tariff flights, and, in this, they are like large hotel groups. The list of products that are aimed at both markets is endless and growing.

The second reason is that the fundamental nature of a product seems to determine the way it is positioned and advertised more than the question of whether the customer is an individual or a company. And virtually all the goods and services companies buy can be fitted into the broad groups we have already analysed in the preceding chapters.

Business buys large quantities of basic, functional goods. For instance, the catering trade buys many of the same products and the same brands that occupy the shelves of high street supermarkets. The same companies that sell cleaning products to the housewife sell similar products in large containers to industrial maintenance companies.

Business also buys high-ticket items – including very high-ticket items like mainframe computers, ocean-going tankers, aircraft, and building projects. And business (and businessmen, buying with company money if partly at least for personal consumption) are as we have seen important customers for conspicuous consumption products and services.

Business buys so much and of such varied nature that it is simply deceptive to suggest that there is one overall, generally applicable way in which business is to be approached. All the indications are that most products are successfully sold in the same broad way, be the target market housewives or industrial or trade buyers.

This does not of course mean that preparing advertising to appeal to the industrial buyer should take no account of the needs of that customer. All successful advertising is successful precisely because it does take cognisance of the customer's needs and predilections. But the industrial or trade buyer will tend to view the same broad categories of product in much the same way as the private customer, simply because they fulfil the same sort of function in his life.

Are there differences? I think there are two:

1. The trade or industrial customer is often a many-headed beast. There are many people involved in the sale whereas in consumer goods the sale is usually made to one individual.

2. The trader by definition, and very often the industrial customer too, is not buying for his own consumption: he is buying with his eye on his own customers.

These two characteristics do have some fairly serious effects. Let us have a look at them.

The effects of group decision making

The many different people who influence the buying decision all have their own particular interests and attitudes that affect that decision, and it is a good thing to understand them.

The buyer is interested in the terms he can procure (since that reflects credit on him), in maintaining a sensible inventory level, in having a minimum of two and a maximum of perhaps four suppliers for ease of administration. If the product is in a category which is seen as critical or 'tricky' in some way, then the buyer will usually play safe. One reason for the remarkable position that IBM enjoyed in the mainframe computer market was a self-reinforcing function of their own success. Buying departments realised that the purchase of a computer was something where they could easily reap major trouble, if – as so often seemed to happen – the machine attracted a lot of adverse comment and criticism when the installation was new. But if they had recommended the market leader they were essentially above criticism. Nobody could say they had taken a foolish decision.

The trade buyer is slightly different in his motivation from the buying agent of an industrial company. He is a major power at most retailers. He is looking for a product that will give him guaranteed sales at profitable prices, and particularly he is looking to limit the goods he has on offer in each department. So his main interest is that the limited range he buys can fill the full demands of the market.

The technical decision maker may very well have nothing to do with the product that is finally delivered, though his specification and tests are absolutely critical to its getting ordered in the first place. He is not particularly interested in price, and, to the annoyance of the rest of the company, absolutely uninterested in the supplier's reliability and promptness of deliveries.

The actual user – the manager of the department that will employ the product you are selling, perhaps as an ingredient in their product, perhaps as a piece of bought-in equipment, perhaps to carry out a manufacturing function – is also concerned that the product meets its specification, but he is also, more than anything else, vitally concerned that it is available when he needs it.

Top management can be very interested in buying decisions or totally uninterested. The soap for the washrooms, the choice of pencils, the packaging materials, these normally leave them cold. But if the decision is a large one, if it is a highly visible piece of equipment or architecture, if its possession confers prestige – then you can be fairly certain that their opinion will be vocal and influential. In the case of high cost equipment that requires a board decision for it to be bought at all, then the influence of the company's financial officer will be considerable – and holding the purse strings he can easily hold the veto. Often the way to appeal to him is to offer him a *better financial way to buy*. Not a price cut.

What we are talking about is shifting the sale, for instance, on to a rental basis as against an out-and-out purchase. This is the secret of the success of contract hire as a means of selling cars and trucks to companies. Such innovative acquisition methods usually only offer a temporary advantage because they cannot be insulated against imitation. Nevertheless, they are an excellent example of a way to position a product to a key decision maker.

In all these situations the key thing is to attempt to identify the most important buying influence and to concentrate your efforts on so positioning the product that it appeals strongly to that customer. Often there is a buyer whose influence greatly outweighs all the others. If your product can be made very appealing to him, then, by virtue of his superior influence, he will bring the others round.

Often, of course, the situation is not so cut and dried. You have to live with the fact that there are several customers to whom you must appeal. Then you have to identify their particular interests and devise a positioning that can either satisfy them all or, at the very least, attract one without repelling others.

The effects of selling to an intermediary

The other characteristic of trade and business-to-business marketing is that the customer you sell to is often not the ultimate customer.

The way to deal with this situation is to attempt to judge who really has the greater influence on the product decision. Generally but not exclusively this is the end customer. You then position your product as strongly as possible to appeal to the end customer, while not making the mistake of totally neglecting your direct customer.

While this has been practised in branded goods for a long time, it is frequently disregarded in industrial marketing.

> A major chemical company producing the plastic used in those little cups that provide the packaging for cream, yoghurt, cottage cheese and so on, suddenly found that its sales were rapidly declining.
>
> Talking to customers – the companies that processed the plastic material and made the little pots – they simply heard that their customers, the dairy companies, were moving to another plastic because it was marginally cheaper. However they were not satisfied with this explanation and tried asking the dairy companies direct.
>
> What they found out there was a totally different story. The dairy companies were changing to another material not because of price but because they found that the other plastic could actually give their

products at least another day's shelf-life in the grocery store. This was of enormous importance to them, since the cost of delivering and uplifting products with a short shelf-life was very high and any increase in store life gave them a great competitive advantage.

The manufacturers of the other plastic material – if they had found out that their product improved shelf life – could actually have sold it at a premium price instead of undercutting the original supplier. The dairy companies would still have insisted on it, so great was this benefit to them. A clear and compelling positioning could have been consciously built up on this basis – as it was, it was only by chance that the dairy industry found out that the new plastic had this great plus.

Focusing on the end customer is no more than the basic theory of branded goods, all of which were originally produced on the principle of providing the consumer with a clearly-profiled, desirable product and knowing that consumer demand would force trade co-operation.

Since those halcyon days for manufacturing industry the trade has got a lot more concentrated and quite a lot tougher and, in the grocery business at least, having reasonable consumer acceptance is no guarantee that you will get stocked.

Though the grocery trade is in the forefront of this development of what Galbraith would call 'countervailing power', there are signs that many other retail markets are going the same way. The concentration in the furniture trade, the drug supermarkets, the increasing concentration in fashions and electric appliances have all already led and will all inevitably lead further to manufacturers having to treat the question of trade acceptance as a major problem.

As more and more retail businesses become concentrated in a few hands, the concomitant effect is increased power in the hands of the large trading groups. This can be used to force prices down, thus enabling the large groups to offer consumer prices that are lower, and ultimately so low that they force hundreds of little corner shops out of business.

However the power of the trade can be used in other ways. If there is some factor which is highly important to traders and not of great moment to consumers, then the trade will usually be able to get its way. The demise of the returnable glass bottle and its replacement by a one-way plastic container or can has come about not because of any strong consumer preference but because the trade has simply refused to carry out the chore of handling bottles.

One outward sign of this increased trade power is a proliferation of private label goods. Manufacturers usually see this (if they can see at all for the rage that blinds them) as the ultimate insult. For the retailer to squeeze their margins, refuse them admittance and then finally come out with his own carbon copy of their merchandise seems insupportable. Yet the retailer *needs* his own goods. Until branded goods were invented retailers were king. It was accepted that you got the best tea at this shop, the best cheese at that shop, the best meat at that shop. It was only the emergence of the brand that put the responsibility for quality into the manufacturers' hands and made the retailer an automaton in the distribution chain.

Consequently the most forward-looking and successful retailers have always wanted their own brands, goods that are theirs and nobody else's, to demonstrate the quality of their shops. It is not suprising that two of the biggest success stories in British retailing, Sainsbury's and Marks & Spencer, have always laid great stress on their own label goods.

Taking account of the trade buyer while positioning a product against the final customer is a tricky business. The obvious solution is to stress the high volume of sales and the high profit that will accrue from handling your product. Yet, factually, your product is often no better than many others in this regard. The one product he probably *needs* is the market leader.

So your positioning job is to make it clear to the trade buyer that your product is in some way *irreplaceable:* that other competing products cannot readily be substituted for it, that customers will demand yours and walk away rather than accept something else.

You can also seek to position the kind of customers you will bring into his store as being especially desirable – free-spending, good customers for other merchandise he has on offer, for instance.

Finally, you can seek to position your product in terms of his financial advantage. This should be a little more sophisticated than simply talking about the sales your product will bring. Very few of the sales new products make in shops are clearly and indisputably incremental.

Mostly they are simply borrowed from other goods that are already in stock – so while the sales of your product are a net gain to you, to a trade customer they may well not represent any additional business. If you can prove sales are incremental, of course, then you have a very strong point. But there are other financial arguments you can use. Can you show a better trade margin than competitors? Can you show faster turnover? Can you do the same sales from a smaller amount of shelf space?

Any of these tactics will aid your sales to the trade customer. But it is important that such a positioning to the intermediate customer does not conflict with your overall positioning to the end customer who is – to repeat – generally to be regarded as more important. Ideally, when you are positioning a product, the trade positioning should complement and strengthen the consumer positioning.

CHAPTER 12

Facts for Effective Advertising

So many books on advertising command you laconically to 'Get all the facts'. That they dispose of this vital exercise in one four-word sentence suggests that the process may be fairly skimpy.

On the other hand the relevant facts about the company, the product, the market, the competition, the trade and the consumer are a vital part of effective advertising. The process of fact collection must take place.

I am aware that by dealing with it in this chapter we rather suggest that the fact-finding process should be carried out at this point – after a positioning has been finalised and at the same time as a copy strategy is in development. Nothing could be further from the truth.

Fact-finding and fact updating are *ongoing processes in the whole business of marketing. It is at this stage however that your evaluation and use of the information you have gathered probably has most effect.*

Let us see how this evaluation can be done most effectively.

Maintaining a fact book

One of the basic weapons of brand managers and marketing managers is that bulging folder they call their fact book. Fundamentally this is a weapon to enable them to answer the unreasonable questions of management without having to go back to their desks. If somebody says, 'What did we sell last year in South Shields?' they can turn it up and answer the question.

The principle of the fact book is a very good one for anybody planning marketing and advertising. Very simply, you keep in one regularly updated, organised file all the key factual information you receive. You keep back information, too, to enable you to follow and detect trends.

Brand managers at large consumer goods companies have the benefit of fairly complex systems of ongoing research and reliable, regular statistics. Others may have to compile their fact books on a more haphazard and *ad hoc* basis. The principle, however, remains the same.

Your fact book should cover:

Sales   Your own sales, ideally in the form of *shipments* – ie the actual amounts physically leaving the factory. Unlike the accountants you are not interested in cash flow, or, like the sales department, in future promises. You want to know how much is actually being bought and consumed by the final customer. Ideally you should have shipment figures that go back for five years and are broken down on a monthly basis.

Some businesses produce sales statistics on a daily basis. This is fine, but it is far too frequent to show trends easily. One big sale can falsify two or three days or more. Always add daily or weekly sales together to produce monthly, or (to even out inequalities in the number of selling days) four-weekly figures.

Shipments should be broken down by area and by product type (for instance if you have two different flavours, or varying package sizes, or different colours or designs). In consumer goods where price-off packs and other deals are common, it is also wise to separate promotional merchandise and regular merchandise. If you work through differing trade channels, then a breakdown of the sales by type of outlet is also valuable.

Measurement of shipments is simplified if *statistical units* are established and compared. For instance, if you sell cases of 24 × ½ lb packs and 12 × 1 lb packs, then the actual cases are strictly comparable in volume, each containing 12 lbs. If, on the other hand, you sell your large size in cases containing only 10, then you will have to multiply those cases by 0.8 to get comparable statistical units.

Such statistics should be on one sheet of paper

and going back three to five years.

You will also want your shipments in value terms. This can be less precise and detailed and simply broken down by quarter.

Consumption

You will want to know what is happening to the entire market – if your sales went up by ten per cent last year but the market as a whole doubled, then probably you have no reason to con-gratulate yourself.

Market size figures are often provided by Government statistics, (where they are usually a year out of date), by retail audits or by trade associations. The retail audit has the advantage of giving more information, particularly of showing individual brand shares. It also has the disadvantage of costing more and not being available for many markets.

Aim to make your general market information as comparable as possible to your own sales statistics. If the market information shows certain areas, then break down your statistics by the same areas. You want as much detail in terms of product variants, areas, trade channels and prices as possible.

Development Indices

These may seem an unnecessary sophistication but they are extremely simple to produce and make comparison of statistics far easier.

The procedure is to express your own sales and the sales of the entire market as a certain number of statistical units per head of population, and then to express this as an index both nationally and area by area. It works like this:

	Sales in statistical units	*Population (000s)*	*Sales: Pop ratio*	*Index*
National	200,000	40,000	5	100
Area 1	5,000	2,000	2.5	50
Area 2	35,000	5,000	7	140
Area 3	10,000	1,500	6.66	133

It will be obvious that the total market sales

can be expressed in this way just as your own sales can. The benefit is that you can see at a glance which areas are performing better than average and which worse than average. You can also see where your low sales are due to the whole market being underdeveloped and where they are due to competitive pressure.

This measurement can be made more meaningful by defining the population for your product more precisely – for instance, taking the population of car owners if you sell an automotive product or the numbers of babies under one year if you sell a baby food.

Distribution

This is an important measurement if you sell through the retail trade – you want to know in what percentage of outlets your product is present (specifying those who stock it, those who are temporarily out of stock) and if this varies by product type and size.

Competition

You should tabulate competitors by size, price, type of product, their trade terms if these are variable and significant, and also note their advertising and promotional expenditure.

If your competitors' products have been subjected to a formal analysis and evaluation, then this should appear here: if this is not available, include your own evaluation of their products. (Try to be objective, you're kidding no-one but yourself.)

Consumer

This should contain all you know about your consumer market – numbers, demographic data, location – and also a summary of any information as to their attitudes and usage habits for your type of product. In markets where your product is sold to a processor or manufacturer who then fabricates it for the final user, then this data should appear for both groups. Their motivations and characteristics are often dramatically different.

Advertising and Promotion

You will want to have full details of your own advertising and promotional plans, your own media plans and also records of what you have done in past years.

It is also desirable that, in addition to your own copy strategy and examples of your ads, you should have those of your major competitors. A useful evaluation of their effectiveness can be achieved by going through the exercise we have carried out in Chapter 13, page 74, and attempting to reconstruct the copy strategy your competitors are using.

Now the fact book is a very desirable thing. But people active in other types of business, with far fewer pieces of formalised research and statistical information at their disposal, are likely to be both flabbergasted at its detail and envious of the amount of information on hand. If your market is simply not so organised, and if the funds to collect information are simply not available, what do you do?

The first thing you do is refuse to give up easily. You can have impeccable information on your own product, sales, advertising and so on, and you have only yourself to blame if you neglect to keep them in a form that makes reference to them simple and revealing.

There are usually more statistics available about competitors and total market size than you might think. For instance, you can:

Measure a related statistic

Nobody records the number of private house sales in the UK annually. But you can get hold of the number of new house completions and the number of mortgages taken out. Getting a clear fix on the information you want by measuring something closely related is a simple and not ineffective way out.

Estimate

Estimate the sales in the market – ideally by approaching it in more than one way. Take the number of dealers, allocate a set turnover per dealer and see what that produces. At the same time, make an estimate of your share of total volume and plus that up to get an estimate of market size. If the two figures don't tally, try to find out why not and seek to reconcile them.

Such estimates are perhaps best expressed not as concrete numbers but as share figures with a sizeable spread. It is important to recognise that these estimates are just estimates and not to treat them as gospel. Any chance to inject a bit of fact into them should be taken. (One tip – the grocery trade is very careful to match shelf space to market turnover. If you compare the shelf space you have with a category whose total size is known you can get a good feel of what your market's size may be. And the number of facings a brand has will certainly reflect that brand's share in that shop at least.)

Do fieldwork

Talking to retailers, to wholesalers, to customers almost always helps you get a better feel for the market – both in its quantitative as well as its qualitative aspects. Any information of a quantitative nature should be fitted into the overall picture you are trying to build up.

Do desk research

There is a suprisingly large amount of information around in published form. There are (usually very expensive) market reports published by research companies. If you can't afford the report, you can at least look about for any reviews of the book that will usually quote statistics. Another fruitful source of confidential information are the annual reports of companies, some of their PR releases, and particularly the very detailed information which is required when a company goes public.

Look at related markets

In all this your real aim is to understand more about your market and your customer. This does not necessarily mean exclusively or even primarily numbers. It means understanding the fundamental dynamics. If there is no information on your market, but there is a host of published information about similar markets then soak yourself in that. You will probably be able to spot the differences quite rapidly and allow for them, and the similarities can be very illuminating.

Talk to chemists and production people

The people who make the product can often give you some very interesting information about why it is the way it is. This can often be the key to developing a sales argument in advertising. Listen carefully and don't be afraid to ask what may seem like obvious questions.

PART TWO

From Positioning to Selling Idea

CHAPTER 13

From Positioning Statement to Copy Strategy

We have dealt with the subject of the fundamental positioning of a product or service because this really is at the heart of using advertising successfully. It is also the part of the task most frequently scamped or ignored.

The next step – the formulation of a copy strategy – is also all too often neglected.

Let us see what these two in fact are:

Positioning statement. This is a description of the long-term position you wish the product to occupy in the mind of the consumer.

Copy Strategy. This is a statement of those beliefs, attitudes and feelings you wish the consumer to have about your product after seeing advertising for it.

People may well have the initial feeling that these two statements add up to the same thing. They do not, but they certainly are very closely and causally related. It is also, in my opinion at least, of considerable benefit to make the distinction between them. All the experience shows that it is at this analytical stage that campaign planning tends to go seriously awry. Any tool that produces clarity and keeps us on course at this stage is to be welcomed.

However, we do have to use the tools as tools. All too often what happens is that someone sits down with a ragbag of facts and opinions called a 'brief' and produces some advertisements. Because everybody likes them and has a confused but general feeling that they are right, they then have to be provided with respectability in the form of strategy back-up. So, after the event, a document is fudged together to justify what has already happened. This is obviously, at the very least, a waste of time. That it can be a justification of thoroughly ineffective advertising is also clear.

Major brands regard their advertising documentation as a kind of state secret and do not publish it. They do however publish the advertising and, from this, it should not be difficult to work our way back to some such documentation as either did or should have existed. We will attempt to do this for two or three well-known products and produce some 'ideal' positioning statements and copy strategies. Perhaps the differences between the two will then become a little clearer.

Example 1: Amstrad

Amstrad Positioning Statement. Amstrad will be positioned as the company that offers 'price-breaking' equipment in the technologically advanced electronic appliance field. The appliances are of excellent quality and are aggressively marketed.

Amstrad 8256 copy strategy
To convince smaller business users and private users that the Amstrad 8256 word processor is a fully equipped word processor at an unprecedentedly low price.

This will be explained by mentioning refinements like the 256K memory, size and capacity of monitor, software package and two-speed printer, together with the availability of the twin disk drive 8512.

All communication will assume that readers have only a nodding acquaintance with word processing and avoid technical jargon, while encouraging them to seek more information, either from retailers or direct from Amstrad.

Let us make a few comments on these, I stress again, invented documents.

First, notice that the positioning statement is a positioning of the company rather than of a specific product. This is logical in the market in which Amstrad operates. The appliances themselves are in fast-moving markets where what is sensationally new this year is standard next year and out of date the year after that. It would be very hard to build individual product positions in such a rapidly moving field.

Figure 12 Amstrad – the ad from which the copy strategy has been reconstructed

Much better to position Amstrad the company as the company from whom sensationally low prices can be expected, regardless of which appliance is being offered.

This price-breaker position is also a logical one for a company that has deliberately set itself up for low-cost overseas production and aims at distribution through high street retailers rather than the specialist office equipment suppliers. The high street can greatly widen the potential market for such appliances, provided the shops can offer a previously specialised appliance at a price that makes it possible for the private user to buy.

The copy strategy, by comparison, is product-specific. It relates to the 8256 word processor and makes a brief mention of another model, the 8512. This is logical, since advertising, for which the copy strategy is a blueprint,will usually tend to be devoted to a specific product. Yet it is in line with the positioning since it requires us to present the product as being sold 'at an unprecedentedly low price'.

The copy strategy also tells the copywriter what support he should use for the claims he makes as to the product. It is a 'well-equipped' word processor and in support he should mention the memory, the monitor, the software package, and the printer, also noting the existence of the twin disk drive product.

Finally the copy strategy gives the copywriter clear indications of the sort of people to whom his ad should be addressed: small business users and private users, with the additional caveat that they do not know much about the technicalities of word processing. We want to direct these people to the high street shops where they will be at home and we want to have the opportunity to give them further details of the machine – which is mirrored in the final advertisement by listing the main high street chains that carry the product and by the incorporation of a coupon.

What the copy strategy does not do is specify the selling idea of the ad, the comparison with the price of a typewriter. This is a creative contribution from the copywriter – and a very powerful one. He has argued that a typewriter is familiar to everybody likely to be in the market for a word processor and that a typewriter is – unlike the word processor – seen as inexpensive. The comparison is particularly appropriate since both machines do much the same job. Obviously, by putting the word processor in the same price bracket as the typewriter it replaces, he establishes very quickly its unprecedentedly low price.

Example 2: Sharwoods Indian Products

Positioning statement
Sharwoods is a comprehensive range of Indian condiments that make it easy to produce genuine Indian dishes.

Copy strategy
To convince cooks ambitious to make Indian dishes that they can easily achieve genuine results with the Sharwoods range of spices, chutneys, rice, bread products etc.

Sharwood's knowledge and expertise and the genuine nature of the products compensate for any inexperience on the part of the cook.

Advertising will depict traditional Indian cooking as varied and desirable and, with Sharwoods' expertise, readily accessible to British cooks.

Here the positioning statement is a product positioning and it states clearly what the Sharwoods products actually are. They are basically fairly simple products, available at modest prices in every supermarket, yet they aim to have the cachet of the 'genuine'.

This is achieved, first of all, by maintaining an otherwise unknown name for them – Sharwoods. The same range could have been marketed under one of the other names from the Rank Hovis Macdougall stable. But Macdougall's curry powder (for instance) would have been rejected by ambitious would-be Indian cooks as a phoney. This is a positioning decision and certainly a right one.

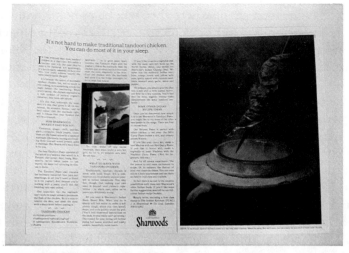

Figure 13 Sharwoods – two examples of a well judged and very successful campaign

In the copy strategy, a careful balance is sought between conveying that the results will be totally genuine while also stressing that the actual cooking is not difficult and does not require special skills.

Apart from insisting on the dual benefits of simple preparation and genuine results, the copy strategy does not tell the creative man to do any of the things that are logically in his bailiwick. It does not tell him to write long and detailed copy – though this is the way he chose to interpret the instruction to 'depict traditional Indian cooking as varied and desirable' and demonstrate 'Sharwoods' knowledge and expertise'. He could have chosen atmospheric pictures of the Taj Mahal, or had the chef at Veeraswamys say that he always used Sharwoods products or

77

done lots of other things. The way that was chosen was longish copy, detailed information and lots of practical little hints that say, 'Come in. Don't be frightened. You can do it.'

It is worth noticing too that a good copy strategy gives the creative man a good feel of the type of person he is addressing. It does not do this in the abstractions of the statistician, talking about C1 and C2 and precise age-groups and urban or rural. Rather it stresses what sort of person the prospect is in relation to the product being sold. Sharwoods aim at all those cooks who like Indian food and have the ambition to produce it at home. They may be well off. They may be in very modest circumstances. They may be AB Colonels' widows brought up 60 years ago in the Raj. They may be just-married typists living in Balham and occasionally going out to the local tandoori restaurant. They have in common a fondness for Indian food and this is really the only characteristic that Sharwoods need to address.

Example 3: Armagnac

Positioning statement

Armagnac, a traditional but little known type of French brandy, will be positioned as the exclusive brandy.

Copy strategy

To establish that Armagnac is an 'in' drink and valued by people who are in the know.

This is because it is France's oldest brandy.

The advertising will appeal to people who like to be one-up on others in their choice of drinks and demonstrate prestige and knowledge.

Unlike the other two examples, we have here a consumer positioning. Armagnac is seeking to increase its popularity by positioning itself against those people who like to drink something that others do not know and thus demonstrate a certain exclusive knowledge.

The copy strategy reflects this fairly simple positioning adequately and seeks to justify the product's stance by stating that it is France's oldest brandy. The execution seems fairly perfunctory to this reader and unlikely to make us a nation of Armagnac drinkers. Particularly, it does not give us any hint as to who these 'best' people are who know about Armagnac, or tell us anything about Armagnac itself. The latter seems a

Figure 14 Armagnac – thin strategic thinking produces thin ads

major failing, because it is hard for people who want to emulate the nobs who drink Armagnac, if they cannot then, when they order it, show off a little knowledge and connoisseurship. Saying it comes from France and has been around a long time, while important facts, are simply not enough.

From these examples it is perhaps a little clearer in what ways a copy strategy differs from a positioning statement. A positioning statement should sum up the product's long-term positioning aim – what the product hopes to be. It is valid usually for the whole life of the product. It affects such basic things as package design and the product name. It should go on and on. It should clarify those – usually very simple – things that are implicit in the product itself.

A copy strategy, on the other hand, is a blueprint for an immediate advertising campaign. It is shorter term. It can aim to deal with a particular competitive situation. It can change and develop logically as the brand develops. It can insist on much greater information being transmitted since it is a guide to words and pictures.

A good copy strategy will usually have three parts: first, it will state what the advertising will aim to convey. It is important that this is understood as what the reader or viewer will get out of the advertising, rather than what we, the advertiser, put in. What understanding of the product, what belief about it should I attempt to communicate?

Second, it will outline the facts that are to be used to support the conviction I am aiming to produce. These are numerous in fairly complex products like the Amstrad and should be listed if they are of strategic importance. If they are simply background and constantly changing as in the Sharwoods campaign, then it is perhaps better to express them in the strategy generally in some such phrase as 'the company's expertise'.

Third, the copy strategy will describe the sort of people the ad should talk to. Not, as we have said, primarily demographically (unless there is demographic limitation on product interest; for instance, only car drivers are really in the audience for cars, only mothers are in the audience for baby food) but in terms of their personalities, interests, habits and aspirations that are relevant to the product sale.

The greatest danger with copy strategies is to write them with a campaign in mind. If the brand has a long-established slogan, it is certainly not unreasonable to mention it and suggest that it should continue to be used. But it is always limiting and dangerous to put creative requirements into a stategy. Statements like 'X will be shown as the chosen brand of youthful, attractive people' more or less require you to depict such people. The better ad may not show anybody at all and still fulfil the strategic intention. For instance, if the price comparison with the typewriter had been put into the Amstrad copy strategy, it would have allowed the ad we have shown, but would have more or less precluded any other equally valid ad. A good copy strategy keeps all the creative options open – while still being totally unambiguous about strategic direction. Writing such documents is not easy and every word should be carefully weighed to make sure no unintentional bias has crept in. If this sort of investment of mental effort and time is put into the copy strategy then it is far less likely to be hurriedly discarded or wantonly changed.

CHAPTER 14

Building a
Copy Strategy

A copy strategy is a fuller document than a positioning statement, as we have seen. It needs to be written with extreme care since it is the bible for a brand's communications effort. Copy strategies are often written on an annual basis but there is no real reason to think that a document will necessarily have become inapplicable simply because the first of January has come round. Essentially a copy strategy should remain the basic document against which a product's advertising should be measured *until there is a valid reason for changing what the brand wishes to communicate.*

The copy strategy is logically based on the positioning statement and should not contradict it. However, there is no reason why a consumer positioning statement should not spawn a product-oriented copy strategy. There will always be the need to communicate product information in advertising – even if it is a statement as thin as 'France's oldest brandy' – and this should be defined in the copy strategy.

Copy strategies, as we have said, can and should change, but when such changes do occur they should ideally be very minor. The basic thrust of a product's communicative effort should be continuous, even though changing market conditions, changes in the competition and other such eventualities can require modifications to the strategy.

There are some basics for writing good strategies.

1. *There should not be more than one central promise.* The first paragraph of the strategy usually says quite clearly what the product will do for the consumer who buys it. There is a promise of a specific benefit that the product will provide. Whenever possible this should be limited to one clear promise. Two or three benefits are a nightmare in communication. It has, in fact, often been shown that 'strengthening' the advertising by adding a secondary promise is usually a disaster. Registration of the main benefit goes down while the secondary

benefit is not registered either – both promises are usually communicated at an unsatisfactory level.

If two benefits are unavoidable a good strategy will connect them logically so that they become one idea. For instance, this is what happens in the strategy we ascribe (very cheekily) to Sharwoods. Because Sharwoods has the knowledge and expertise, and has built these into their products, cooking genuine Indian food is easy for you.

2. *Make sure the central promise is a promise.* All too often strategies get written that make no promise at all. They say what the product is. They tell us perhaps what the consumer should do. The first paragraph of a strategy should always say, in effect, 'This product will give you this specific benefit.' And the benefit must be consistent with and based on the positioning statement.

3. *Make sure the promise is exclusive.* We cannot always say 'only X will give you this benefit'. But we can often say that X will provide the benefit to a greater degree than its competitors. Or we can in various other ways imply exclusivity, for instance by pointing out that our product was the first to provide this benefit. Or provides it to more people than any other. Or provides it at lower cost, or with greater convenience, or with some other point of exclusivity.

4. *Support the promise.* This is usually the matter of the second paragraph of the strategy. It says why the reader can be sure the promise in the first paragraph can in fact be delivered. Support can take many forms – for instance, we can adduce some product ingredient or feature in the product. We can claim greater care in manufacture or better fundamental design.

Alternatively a promise can be supported not by the way the product is made but by demonstrating that it can do what we say, or by adducing some kind of independent testimony.

The whole matter of support is largely dependent on how competitive and crowded the market is and how similar consumers perceive products to be. If the market is full of essentially similar products then an understandable, convincing support for what may well be a fairly generic claim will be most urgent. If the market is less crowded and products are more distinctive, this urgency is greatly reduced.

5. *Define the consumer addressed.* We have covered this point already. The

person who is the target of the advertising should be defined as a consumer of the product concerned.

6. *Make sure priorities are clear.* There is no harm in insisting on quite large amounts of subordinate information in a strategy, as long as this is clearly recognised as subordinate. It must be clear that this is not to impede communication of the central promise.

Perhaps the most useful way to think of a strategy is as a description of what you would hope the ideal consumer would play back to you if asked what you were saying in your advertising. It is not the words you say, but the ideas you hope your customers understand and believe.

This approach to a copy strategy is also helpful when attempting to isolate the ideal promise and the best support for it.

It is of course unlikely that you would have gone through the work of positioning the product and not have a good feel for what fundamental promises would be effective in the market. Positioning is a matter of looking at the market through the consumer's eyes, and the product that is clearly and well positioned will generally have its central promise automatically prescribed for it.

The support for a particular promise is always important and, again, it can often be found by trying to look through the consumer's eyes. Ask yourself, 'What would make me believe that this claim was true?'

Support for a promise can come from all sorts of areas and the only real restrictions are that it is

a.   interesting;
b.   inherently believable.

Seeking support, you can find it:

In the product itself

In its ingredients; method of manufacture; the qualifications of the people who make it, who designed it, who test it; how fresh it is; how mature it is; how much hand labour is in it; how faultlessly automated the production process is.

In the people who make it

The oldest established firm; the newest and most go-ahead; the biggest; not a factory but a farm, a cottage industry; the location –

rural, in a particular country, in a particular climate; particularly dedicated workers because of the way they are paid or recruited or because of their culture.

In its packaging

Its convenience; its ability to protect the product better; its second uses; its more practical sizes; the substance it is made of.

In the way it is sold

Through a different channel of distribution; delivered fresher and quicker; on more attractive terms; at especially good shops; more responsive to consumer complaints or suggestions.

In its actual performance

The product or a vital ingredient subjected to tests – either in everyday use or exaggerated torture tests; comparative tests against competitors; reports from users in demanding areas.

In the people who buy it

Particularly knowledgeable users, or particularly heavy users; perhaps they are unusually loyal to it; perhaps they use it to do especially exacting or difficult or important tasks.

In the opinion of others

Do independent judges rate it highly? Are competitors specially wary of it? Does it have imitators?

This list does not pretend to be exhaustive, but it should go some way to answering the moans of those who say 'There's nothing different about this product'.

CHAPTER 15

Introducing the Selling Idea

I am aware that we have got a good way into this book and have barely spent a sentence on clever slogans, attractive pictures, intriguing headlines and all the other highly creative things that advertising seems to consist of.

There is a reason for this. All the formal experience that has been gathered tends to show that *content is more important than style*. What you say is more important than how you say it.

It is hardly surprising. I suggest you take an honest look at your own buying behaviour, and I think you will find you generally choose the product that seems to suit you best, rather than buying something that seems less appropriate simply because you want to pay tribute to the cleverness of its advertising.

Most writers on advertising acknowledge this fact by saying – before they get on to the much more fascinating slogans and things – 'Get all the facts'. This begs the questions of what facts you need, how they should be organised and how they should be interpreted. We hope, that by spending so long on fundamental positioning practice, and then showing how this can lead to a logical copy strategy, some of this will have become clear. 'Getting the facts' means understanding the role the type of product or service in question plays in the life of the consumer, understanding the position the product occupies in relation to its competitors, and finally being able to detect how these relationships can be modified or exploited for the benefit of the product the health of which we are entrusted with.

But when we have done that the job, of course, is just beginning.

Let us say we have defined the position we wish our product to enjoy. Let us assume we have developed out of that positioning a clear and, we believe, an effective copy strategy. We now have to communicate the results of our efforts to those people who form our logical consumers.

This involves transforming our strategy into a *selling idea*. But what exactly is a selling idea and why is it necessary to have optimum communication?

A selling idea is the unique, memorable and therefore communicable encapsulation of the strategy.

'Fairy Liquid is a dishwashing liquid that is very mild to hands' is strategy.

'Now hands that do dishes can feel soft as your face' is a selling idea.

'ReadiBrek is better for children on cold mornings than cold cereals' is strategy.

'Central heating for kids' is a selling idea.

'The Midland Bank is more sensitive to the needs of its customers' is strategy.

'The listening bank' is a selling idea.

But surely, it can be urged, the positioning statement or the strategic aim can simply be used directly without expressing it in a way that a Devil's advocate might call 'artificial' or 'unduly complex'. If you want to say 'we are more sensitive to the needs of our customers' why not say just that? Why wrap it up?

There are two points that need to be made in any answer to this question.

The first is to ask you to understand the awesome job advertising faces in its task of communicating. The number of commercial messages a so-called 'average' consumer faces in a typical day have been variously estimated at 1,000 to 2,500. The numbers are very hard to prove and clearly vary a lot depending on whether (for instance) you drive to work listening to the local commercial radio station, and along a road with a lot of hoardings. But we can readily agree that the competition for our attention is staggeringly great.

In this competition, ideas that have that element of novelty and memorability that causes them to hook into the mind and become difficult to dislodge are worth their weight in gold. The three sentences we quote above have all managed to penetrate our consciousness against all the odds. It is very likely that the simple statements that precede them – even had they been exposed to the same repetition – would not have done so.

The second point is that a good selling idea is not 'more complex', is not 'artificial'. If it is really good it is in fact quicker and easier to assimilate and understand than the simple statement. Very good ideas of this kind – and, although the entire industry spends much of its time seeking them, they are still as rare as gold dust – stand in the same relationship to the positioning statements behind them as poetry does to prose.

It should not be thought that such selling ideas are necessarily expressed in words. The selling idea is what it says it is – an idea. That idea can just as well be a picture – like the glass and a half of milk in Cadbury's Dairy Milk. It can be a song. To take another example from Cadbury's, would the Fudge words be in any way memorable without their accompanying tune?

A selling idea is a transmutation of the strategy into something unique, memorable and succinct. Being hard-packed and firm, it has the power to penetrate indifference and inattention. Being sharp and finely honed, it can cut through the visual and verbal clutter. Copywriters devising selling ideas are recommended to follow the advice of Andrew Marvell to his coy mistress:

> Let us roll all our strength, and all
> Our sweetness, up into one ball …

The selling idea should communicate quickly and clearly. It should also go on communicating. It should not be something we grow tired of. It should have the potential of becoming part of the language, part of the culture. These are ambitious demands – and only a tiny percentage of advertising ideas do in fact do all this. But, make no mistake about it, those are the ones that really pay off.

The need for a really unique and powerful selling idea is thrown into relief by the fast-moving nature of the marketplace today. Any new product is usually exposed to immediate imitation.

Let us assume that you have just introduced a new product – for the sake of argument, let us suppose it is an instant coffee with its own creamer already incorporated in it. What happens? Competitors who feel themselves threatened incorporate the same ingredient in their products. If the new product starts to take off, then it is rapidly followed by me-too products from every major manufacturer and almost immediately afterwards by private label products that duplicate it as closely as they legally dare.

Now, in this cut-throat world, you are a lot less likely to establish your coffee with in-built creamer effectively and profitably on the market if you simply say:

> Brand So-and-so – the instant coffee
> with its own creamer built in.

That statement – which might well be your positioning statement, might indeed say succinctly if somewhat unimaginatively what you wish to communicate – can undoubtedly be used word for word by any me-too product that follows you. It is also essentially undistinctive. While it may communicate what the product is and what it does, it does nothing to make you remember this product if there are four or five similar products on the supermarket shelf.

This used not to matter in the days when a unique product had perhaps years to establish itself (though even then wise marketers tried to build uniqueness and memorability for their products). Nowadays, when you may only have a few months, when your competitors may be able to spend more money than you, when they may even beat you to national distribution if you have started out in a test market, such lack of uniqueness and distinctiveness matters very much indeed.

We shall look at the techniques behind effective selling ideas in the next few chapters.

CHAPTER 16

How to Build the Selling Idea into the Product

You may have noticed a significant change that has come over new products lately.

Companies, guided by their lawyers, tended in the past to choose meaningless names for their products confident that, in the leisurely tempo of those times, the name could ultimately be filled with meaning. And, of course, it was registrable. Kodak is a typical example. Now, because of the far faster tempo of innovation – and the tempo of imitation which is just as fast or faster – it is becoming clear that the best new product is one that carries its selling idea blazoned on its chest.

> Richardson Vicks invented a night-time cold remedy which they launched with great success in America under the name of Nyqyuil. The same product was launched in Europe as Medinite in Britain and Medinait in Germany. However, in Britain a major competitor, Beecham, got into the market at virtually the same time as Vick. They had the same product, they had much the same advertising story – and they had a name that conveyed the product's selling idea significantly better – Night Nurse.
>
> Starting at the same time, it seems to have been the better name that won out. Night Nurse has now pushed Medinite aside. The inevitable second stage is when the successful product gets aped by a retailer who produces an own label version. Boots – who control some 50 per cent of the pharmaceutical business in Britain, a uniquely high concentration – came out with a product called Nighttime Cold Comfort.

Speed is of the essence. A product that says very clearly what it is about and why you should buy it can much more readily be understood and bought.

Does it matter that it is not registrable? (Names that contain the selling idea are, by definition, not meaningless fabrications but readily

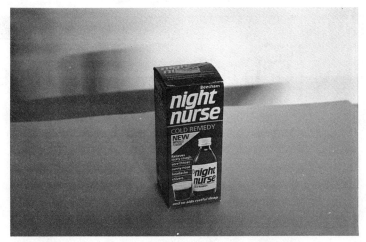

Figure 15 Night Nurse – did the product's name play a big part in its success?

understandable, communicative devices. This means that they will frequently not be able to be registered.) Well, it matters much more to have a product that succeeds rather than to have a cast-iron registration for a product which is a flop. But names that do contain the selling idea can, if they are too close to a generic statement of what the product does or is, be challenged and become common property. McCain's Oven Chips, a very successful example of exactly what we are talking about, has had to live with the fact that its brand name Oven Chips can be used by any of its competitors. Miller Lite, the beer that chalked up tremendous gains in the US leading a move to lighter beers has had to settle for the fact that its brand name is just an alternative spelling of a generic quality.

> After Eight is probably the most successful new introduction in the boxed chocolate market since Black Magic appeared before the War. It is very different from the milk chocolate assortments that were making the running till then, being of plain chocolate, all one flavour, and not depending on the gift usage which has traditionally been crucial to all chocolates.
> Notice how perfectly the name After Eight explains the brand's positioning. It says clearly that this is something for after dinner use – and thus defines the product as for people who eat dinner in the evening rather than at midday. The specific time, eight o'clock, makes it something for formal entertaining and not in any way for children. The name does not specify or even hint at the flavour – mint – thus leaving a line extension open. (Rowntree has, probably very wisely, always eschewed one, but the possibility had to be considered at the launch

91

Figure 16   After Eight – a fine product, excellently named

phase.) Yet the name has nothing banal about it in the way that Dessert Mints, for instance, or some such similar fabrication would have. It could equally well be the name of a play or a book.

Finally, anyone who wants to ape the success of After Eight finds that the name does not help him at all. He is left with rather clumsy generics such as the one we have cited above. He can scarcely call a me-too product 'After Half Past Seven'.

And what if you want to change your product radically? Isn't a name that sums up the selling idea – that in effect *is* the selling idea – a handicap?

Yes, it is. However, brands today have shorter lives and have to be more functionally tied to their markets. It seems rather unlikely that too many of the brands invented in the last few years will still be going strong in fifty years time – which brands like Bisto, Oxo, Kit-Kat, Typhoo and Persil demonstrably are. There is a tradeoff between faster establishment in the market today and a longer, perhaps more variable life generations later. Most marketing directors are determinedly looking for success now, knowing that the future may never materialise.

So far we have talked of brands that use their brand name to transmit their selling idea. It is one step further, one step towards greater uniqueness, to attempt to express the selling idea through the whole package.

In what is appetisingly called 'the yellow fats market', butter is still regarded as 'best' by most consumers, though margarines and dairy spreads (those products that combine some butter, some vegetable fat and perhaps some cream to produce a spread which is lighter dietetically

Figure 17   The unique package shape stresses Golden Churn's butter affinities

and also somewhat cheaper) have recently made significant inroads. The taste and image of butter still rules the roost and manufacturers of other fats are severely limited in what they can claim. Making direct comparisons with the taste of butter is taboo. Kraft – a comparatively small contender in a market dominated by Unilever – has recently had a remarkable success with Golden Churn. While this is a good name in itself and makes use of butter imagery without infringing the restrictions, the product's success is greatly helped by its tub which has been designed to look like a churn, thus giving the product a unique appearance among the rectangular slabs that fill the dairy cabinet of your supermarket and carrying its selling idea right through to the point of sale.

There are a number of other products that have built their selling idea right into the package form – the Jif lemon is a perfect example. Janitor, the US 'industrial strength cleaner' that comes in a drum-styled container, is another. The technique is particularly strong because names can always be imitated to a certain extent, but plagiarism in the package form is usually simply too blatant. The only problem is that the special package can become too idiosyncratic and too 'twee'. For instance, Bell's Whisky are probably right to sell their product in a pottery bottle that looks like a handbell at Christmas. They are also almost certainly right not to go to this form of packaging 100 per cent.

We have already noted how services often enjoy great visibility – shops have extensive premises in busy high street positions, airlines have massive aircraft carrying their livery, pubs and restaurants are products you actually enter and spend time in. It is remarkable that, though they

Figure 18 Janitor used packaging to convey its positioning as an industrial strength cleaner for the home

usually spend large sums on ensuring a clear branding and a corporate identity, they do very little to suggest a selling idea in their premises. Positioning is usually limited to such very simple dimensions as modern/traditional, upmarket/downmarket. The various names in the Conran empire manage to convey clear personalities at least, but there it stops.

Yet the possibilities of conveying a selling idea to customers in an environment that is totally controlled are immense – and almost always ignored. The banks spend millions telling us they are friendly – and put stereotyped, remote and grimly unpleasant interior design behind exteriors which are less welcoming than Fort Knox. How often, when you are inside a supermarket, is it even clear which one you are in? How often, if you fly frequently, have you been uncertain which airline you were on? Identification should not be left to the air-sickness bag alone.

The possibilities of communicating a selling idea are by no means limited to advertising. All the other means have the great advantage of being considerably cheaper. And making the effort to see how it can be done effectively is usually all that is needed to produce real benefits. Finally, communicating your selling idea at the actual point of sale –

through a brand name, a package, through the premises, through stationery, through all the means open to you – is a powerful antidote to your expensive advertising being falsely identified with someone else, a problem that is disquietingly frequent.

CHAPTER 17

What Makes a Powerful Selling Idea?

It is remarkable that selling ideas vary dramatically in effectiveness. Even where the positioning is spot-on, a more effective selling idea can increase the effectiveness of advertising impressively. Ideas that can build big brands are very rare in the welter of advertising that surrounds us but just about every campaign that people remember and talk about has such an idea. Here are a few examples.

Heineken refreshes the parts other beers cannot reach is, if you like, a fairly crazy statement. Yet I am inclined to think that this is a truly remarkable selling idea.

It has, first, that sort of oddity that helps you remember it. It talks about the product being refreshing – which is anything but unusual in the beer field – but makes a claim of superiority (which is traditionally

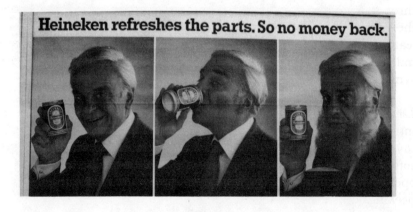

Figure 19 Heineken – when you have an advertising classic you can afford to play games with it

very hard in such a subjective area as refreshment) and puts the idea of refreshment into terms that are unfamiliar and intriguing. The idea is capable of visual interpretation and of an apparently inexhaustible number of them, as we have seen, so there is no doubt of its long-term viability.

Krona Margarine. This was a campaign that never seemed to produce a clear verbal statement of what it was trying to say – the reason presumably lies in those Jesuitical restrictions that make it impossible to talk about butter when you are trying to say that your product tastes like it. But the campaign was remarkably successful and undoubtedly communicated what it set out to communicate. The news style was refreshingly different and the absence of the 'yum-yum' shot where someone – often a child – smacks its lips and takes large bites of the product was a refreshing change.

Marlboro Country. Here the selling idea lies much more in the pictures than the words – yet you could easily imagine this campaign on radio. The essential gambit, positioning a cigarette as masculine by featuring a particular, very masculine environment, certainly wasn't new. In the days when cigarette ads in Britain had much more possibilities open to them, the manly world of the Royal Navy was a favourite and had two brands vying for it, Players Navy Cut and Senior Service, which were the two most successful brands in the country. What has made Marlboro so remarkable is their restraint. They have identified their cowboy world and they have stuck to it through thick and thin. They have resisted every temptation to 'widen the appeal' by showing city slickers down on the ranch, or by featuring the occasional cowgirl. This restraint – and many, many millions of dollars – has given them sole rights to a great, worldwide symbol.

Lenor's 'Conscience' campaign. Lenor was the first fabric softener to be introduced in Germany and it was obviously open to the temptation to say very simply and directly what the product did. It made clothes softer in the rinse cycle. Equally obviously such a statement would be open to duplication by other fabric softeners which were already peeking over the horizon.

It was realised that, compared with a detergent which was obligatory for washing, a fabric softener was an optional extra. Yet a fabric softener gives clothes washed in automatic machines much more pleasant wearing qualities and can also be a vehicle for perfume. A campaign was developed that showed the housewife's conscience questioning her on the overall excellence of her wash and recommending Lenor. With this selling idea that has run for decades, Lenor has maintained its brand leadership in the fabric softener market in Germany, while the usage of fabric softener there is the highest in the world.

Persil washes whiter. 'This is a selling idea?' I hear you complain. Surely that is the flattest, straightest product claim, unenlivened by the slightest imagination, that ever existed.

Not so. In fact, washing powders do not wash white. They wash clean. Women got used to judging the overall cleanness of their wash by the whiteness of the white wash – particularly in the days when all bed linen, most towels and most men's shirts were white and the white wash was a big part of the whole. Persil was the first to notice this phenomenon and translated it into a very simple idea illustrated by the happy person in white contrasted directly with the concerned person in off-white. A heavy calibre detergent war, with just about every brand talking whiteness, tended to mask Persil's cleverness in this field but – carpers please note – Persil came out of it with the brand leadership that they had had going in virtually unscathed.

'*Put a tiger in your tank*'. It is modish to sneer at campaigns like Esso's tiger but it was incontrovertibly a dramatic success for Esso and in a market where consumer interest is low and advertising's ability to shift brand shares seems to be quite small. I am also prepared to bet that it is one of the very few campaigns that you can name for petrol and just about the only one that you can tie to the brand name that sponsored it.

Having looked at a few selling ideas we all know, let us see if we can decide what makes them so special.

1. *They reflect the positioning.* This may seem a very obvious, not to say inconsequential remark. When you see, however, how much advertising money is spent on publicising things that have nothing to do with the product's positioning, it is paramount to insist that any selling idea – as a first and, indeed, obvious requirement – *must* reflect the brand's positioning.

2. *They are distinctive*. It is obviously good if you can position your product in a way which is distinctive. This is not always possible. Often there is one key issue in the market and it is how you relate your product to this issue that decides your success. 'How does it taste in comparison to butter?' is the one question every bread spread must face up to. 'How clean does it wash?' is the one question asked of every detergent. In such markets you may have to share a positioning common to, or, at the very best, extremely similar to your main competitors. Having a totally distinctive way of reflecting that positioning is of immense value in such circumstances.

3. *They are concrete – and often visual*. If your selling idea is able to be seen rather than just recounted it often has considerable advantages.If it is not visible, however, it should try to be concrete rather than abstract.

4. *They are long-term and memorable*. A selling idea can work for a product for decades and only get stronger all the time. It should be able to be incorporated into all sorts of differing campaigns. It should work in all media.

Now, obviously a selling idea will simply go on getting stronger and increasing its recognition with repetition. But a really good one should have that uniqueness and distinctiveness that leads to it being remembered the very first time anybody sees it.

5. *They relate to the consumer*. A selling idea that reflects a product positioning will, of course, be product-oriented. But it will usually not fail to express that orientation in a way that is full of consumer relevance.

CHAPTER 18

The Art of Communication

Peter Drucker recounts the old riddle asked by the Buddhists and the Rabbis of the Talmud, 'Is there a sound in the forest if a tree crashes down and there is no one around to hear it?'

The answer is 'No'. True, the tree, falling, sets up sound waves in the air, but it takes the human ear to convert those waves into a discernible noise.

This is a simple but humbling riddle for would-be communicators to remember. *Communication takes place in the ear of the listener, not in the mouth of the speaker.*

So, since communication is at the heart of successful advertising, it is rarely sufficient simply to say what it is that our copy strategy wishes us to communicate. Why not? Because simply saying it does not often result in it being truly communicated. We generate the required sound waves but the ears that should hear are deaf.

One might well ask, why? Why is the simple statement not heard, registered, believed and acted upon? There are a number of reasons:

a. *The noise level in the marketplace is simply too high* and our weight is too small. Fundamentally, this could be cured simply by spending more money and buying more media weight. Unfortunately guaranteeing the media weight you need is often more expensive than the product can afford.

b. The story may be heard but it may well *not be ascribed to our product or service*. We may be saying the right thing – but if we are not communicating the fact that *we* are saying it we are wasting our money.

c. The story *may not be understood*. Copywriters often have a fatal fascination with things that are subtle and indirect. The cunning implication however can often remain a total mystery to the average reader or viewer.

d. The story may simply *not be believed*. This is particularly likely to happen in functional branded goods. The auditor reacts to a welter of essentially similar advertising by saying, 'That's what they all say.'

e. *The story may not last all the way to the store.* How often do we find advertising stories relevant and interesting, yet the intention to buy decays before we actually put it into practice?

So how can we be sure that we actually are going to put our story into the consumer's mind, that we really are going to communicate and not merely to say something that doesn't get through?

Communication, as we have seen, does not seem to have much to do with decibels or point-size in type. Neither does it seem to be able to be bought by glaring colours and star-bursts. (Which I suppose is encouraging since otherwise, the prerogative of communicating with consumers would belong exclusively to the advertiser with the largest budget.) It is not easy to isolate and define the factors that contribute to effective communication, but I believe that the following five are very often vital:

1. *The inherent interest of the subject matter and its relevance for the auditor.*
It has long been known that certain types of pictures are apparently of high inherent interest while others are lower. Cars tend generally to attract male eyes, fashions to attract female eyes, babies to attract women and so on.

From this fact, it is only a tiny jump to note that similar rules apply to particular types of product – there are products whose advertisements command a lot of attention and other products whose advertisements are less regarded. This is largely independent of the way in which the individual advertisement is constructed. It is as though a secret subliminal inspection of the advertisement takes place before it has consciously been seen at all. This subliminal observer ascertains the subject matter of the advertisement and then decides either that it will be ignored, or that it will be commended to the conscious brain.

The subliminal observer is worldly-wise and up to all the tricks of the trade. For instance, he is rarely fooled by the attempts of industrial advertisers to attract his attention with a curvaceous, scantily-clad cutie and then trick him into reading about somebody's nuts and bolts.

While it is often reasonable to talk of 'high interest' and 'low interest' products, it is important to realise that there is always a minority to whom the low interest product is a high interest one – and there are circumstances that change interest levels. (Plumbing is not a high interest subject but to plumbers it is one. And it can become of very great interest to someone normally not interested if he has a catastophic burst and water pouring down the stairs.)

Genuine relevance to the needs and interests of the auditor is almost always honoured. People are necessarily self-centred and they treat the media in a self-centred way. They buy newspapers that reflect their own political persuasion, for instance. They ask first about any product, what will it do for *me*? Relating the product to their needs and interests is the key and central factor in communicating.

2. *Whether the auditor can fit the new information into an established and coherent pattern.* We have standardised and formalised ways of looking at things and understanding what products do for us. We believe, for instance, that a cold has to 'come out', it is dangerous to 'bottle it up' – so the consequence is that a cold remedy that literally eliminated all cold symptoms immediately would be regarded with very great suspicion and scepticism. We believe that the use of labour-saving products is not totally without problems – even if they are factually indistinguishable they are not so 'good'. We believe that cleaners that clean efficiently are automatically rough on hands. There is no end to the beliefs and myths that populate our minds and a piece of communication that seems to offend against these will often be rejected. On the other hand, if the communication uses the *Gestalt* which exists and fits itself into it it will often benefit from it.

3. *Whether the auditor had some hand in discovering the new information himself.* It is a truism that that information you discover for yourself sticks. You have had the thrill of actually finding out – and this is always connected with the information in your mind. With information that was taught in school you only have the boredom of the classroom to remember.

4. *Whether the new information in some way engages the emotions or not.* It is a commonplace that one can be considerably more affected by a drama-tised piece of fiction than by much more harrowing factual events. The

reason is that the skill of writer, producer, actor make Lear's predicament (for instance) plastic and real to you whereas the brief, impersonal statistics about road deaths remain statistics. If you can invest the information with an emotional, personal content, then it is more likely to be communicated.

5. *The existence of an element of what I can only call 'fascination' which results in the information being remembered.* I realise that this is imprecise and almost impossible to evaluate – nevertheless it is often central to communication.

Why is it that the nursery rhymes you learnt years ago still echo in your mind when so many other worthier and more important things have been forgotten? Why is it that the line 'I'd walk a mile for a Camel' stuck in people's minds for years after it had vanished from the hoardings? Why is it that so many people still know that Friday Night is Amami Night?

Some of the most effective advertising has this quality of sticking in the mind because of something incantatory and rhythmic in its words, because of something slightly odd and distinctive in its visuals, because of a tune that you can't get out of your head.

How do you define this quality? Inevitably one is reduced to defining it in terms of itself. It remains in the memory because it has something memorable about it. There is no sure way to find out if a phrase is actually one of those very few that become part of the language. When it happens it is of untold value.

PART THREE

The Advertising Campaign

CHAPTER 19

The Media for Your Message

We have now (some readers, I am sure, are drawing breath and muttering, 'Finally...') reached the point at which we can start planning an advertising campaign. In other words we have left the broad, long-term questions and are asking ourselves, what do we actually do today and tomorrow to advertise our enterprise.

Without any exhaustive recapitulations, it is worth remembering that we have, to reach this stage:

First, defined the position our product occupies in the market.

Second, by studying the market environment and the consumer's attitudes, defined the position that we would like to occupy.

Third, developed and refined our broad ideas about positioning into a clear and detailed copy strategy.

Fourth, distilled out of our copy strategy a strong, long-term selling idea.

We are now ready to confront the waiting masses with this idea and this immediately brings us face to face with the question of media.

This is not primarily or even secondarily a book about media, a subject which has become more and more refined over recent decades, combining some very serious and complex statistical and mathematical work with some very hard-nosed bargaining. Even so, the fundamentals of media are simple and known. It is with those that we will concern ourselves in this one short chapter.

Perhaps the first point that needs to be made is that your enterprise, like all others, will be seeking a specific audience of potential *customers*. And the nature of your business will decide if those customers are

a.   Large, generalised groups of people, such as housewives, car owners, businessmen, children.

b.   Smaller, more specific groups like accountants, squash-players, theatregoers, yacht-owners.

c.   And finally, regardless of whether they belong to a or b, to be approached on a nationwide basis or on a local basis.

It is not always realised that this simple division brings with it the obligation to use one of two fundamentally different types of media. If your target audience is generalised and your scope is national, you can select the mass media: TV, national newspapers, national magazines. If your audience is still generalised but local then you will almost certainly want to use local media – your local newspaper, your local radio station, perhaps your local TV station (though often that will be uneconomic since it will be covering a much larger area than you will be appealing to).

If your audience is specialised, then you will almost certainly want to use specialised media (fundamentally magazines) which approach that specialised audience. Such magazines are essentially national (they may even be international), and the local versions, if they exist at all, are fairly amateurish affairs.

If your business compels you to use local and specialised media you will find that there is a paucity of choice and a dearth of facts about such media which will both frustrate you and limit your advertising sophistication. The principles we are enunciating in this chapter still apply, but the factual basis which their sophisticated use requires may very well be hard to establish.

That said, we should perhaps look first at some key media concepts. The media planning function employs a number of simple concepts which need to be understood.

Target audience. This is the group or groups defined in demographic terms that we consider most likely to be customers for our product, and hence the logical target of our advertising.

Reach. This is the percentage of the target audience reached during a defined time period – usually the period of the planned campaign. This is frequently refined to *effective reach* – the percentage who see a predetermined minimum number of advertisements.

Frequency. The number of times the target audience sees the advertisement. This is usually measured in OTS, a convenient abbreviation for opportunities to see.

Now it will be obvious that calculations of this type can only be made if sound statistical information is on hand. In fact, as we have indicated, the availability of good statistical information is distinctly variable. Such information is usually provided by the media themselves and used as a selling tool by them. This inevitably means that those media that cover large audiences and can charge high rates – for instance, TV and national newspapers – tend to have better and more complete information than the mass of journals that aim at specialised groups. Local media also tend to have little or nothing other than a statement of their circulation available. Partially this is due to their monopoly position in their market, partially it is simply because the financial resources to collect the information (and arguably also the ability of local advertisers to make effective use of it) tend to be limited.

Information is also collected by the advertising community and, because such research needs to be constant and ongoing if it is to be of value, and because it is by no means cheap, it also tends to be restricted to major media. Major media of course use audience information to sell their particular type of medium over others as well as their particular publication. Local and trade markets however are as we have noted often monopoly markets. There is no useful comparison and no alternative choice. So there is little stimulus for either party to collect information that would facilitate that choice.

The question is further complicated by the difficulty of defining media coverage in the case of certain media – posters, for instance, cover large numbers of people but the composition of the audience is almost impossible to define and the relationship of audience member to medium is certainly not as intensive as the relationship between a newspaper and its reader or a TV set and its viewer.

We will consider, first, the most important media available to you and attempt to list their main characteristics, positive and negative:

TV

+   High coverage
Regional flexibility
Outstanding creative impact

−   High cost
High production costs
Short message life
Limited copy opportunity

Newspapers

+   Extreme flexibility
Extended copy opportunity
Low production costs
Extremely high coverage
Durable message
Local and national

−   High cost if used widely
Passive readership
Limited creative impact

Magazines

+   Demographic selectivity
Durability of message
Extended copy opportunity

−   Slow exposure build-up
Little geographic flexibility
Limited creative impact

Radio

+   Low unit cost
Low absolute cost
Low production cost
Regional flexibility

−   Low reach
No visual impact
Short message life

Cinema
+   High unit impact
      Geographic flexibility
      Demographically selective

−   High unit cost
      Low coverage

Outdoor
+   Regular exposure
      Geographically flexible
      Creative impact

−   Short message
      Passive impact

These, then, are the tools the media planner has to deal with. His job consists essentially of five steps:

Step 1 Defining the target audience.
Step 2 Selecting the most appropriate type of media to approach that audience: this we call the *inter-media choice*.
Step 3 Balancing the conflicting demands of reach and frequency.
Step 4 Selecting the right publications etc. within the chosen media group. This we call the *intra-media choice*.
Step 5 Planning for either continuous advertising or a pattern of 'bursts'.

Let us consider these five steps.

Target audience definition

It will be clear that the target audience definition is likely to have been made, in principle at least, before the media planner even comes on the scene. This will generally be an obvious extension of one's planned target customer group and will share the same demographic characteristics, geographical location and so on. At most, they may vary because one may decide to approach people shortly before they become consumers – for instance, by contacting school leavers when one's target audience is in fact university students.

However, you will almost always have the problem of reconciling your target audience definition arrived at from marketing parameters, with the statistics on readership and viewership that the media may be able to offer you. This is particularly difficult in the case of local media where usually only the broadest demographic data are available. In the case of products with very specific types of audience it is also a problem.

The inter-media choice

The choice of the media group or groups to be used is a decision which is dictated by many different considerations. All major media offer the possibility of covering more or less any demographic group more or less fully – the only exception is cinema, which only offers broad reach in the younger age groups. So it is not usually the case that any of the major media groupings are chosen on the basis of their reach alone. However budgetary considerations can put the sole or even partial use of a major medium (TV is the obvious example) out of court even if it is the ideal medium on every other count – in fact, TV is increasingly becoming unaffordable for even major advertisers. If the minimum number of contacts you feel you require to generate a response is simply unaffordable, then you may well decide to forget the medium. Alternatively you may decide to use it but get the frequency you need via another cheaper medium.

Creative requirements obviously have a major role to play in the inter-media choice. If good quality colour reproduction is considered important, then this may well eliminate newspapers (but bring them back in the form of the Sunday colour supplements). If the need to tell a lengthy copy story is important then this may well indicate newspapers and magazines and militate against the use of posters or radio.

Other factors – perhaps we can describe them best as tactical – are also influential. Do you want to impress the trade and enlist their support? They tend to be much more impressed by some media (TV and local media) than they are by others (women's magazines, cinema). Do you want to confront your competitors in the same media that they use? Or do you feel that you can do better by avoiding them and speaking through totally different media – and in part at least to totally different people?

Reach and frequency

The question of reach versus frequency is constantly being canvassed and there are very vocal exponents of both points of view. It is clear that you can hardly sell to people whom you do not reach, so any reach limitation is an automatic limitation of total market size. On the other hand, broad coverage with no repetition behind it will hardly be very effective, particularly if the aim is to attract customers from a competitor. Generally, these are the situations in which reach tends to be emphasised:

Broad, undefined audience
Rapidly expanding market
New product in launch phase
Strong consumer loyalty to product
Low consumer use-up rate
Announcements with high news value

On the other hand, these are the situations that tend to lay the emphasis on frequency:

Rapid consumer use-up rate
Strong loyalty to competitive brand(s)
Highly seasonal products
Complex message to be communicated and assimilated.

The intra-media choice

Once the one or two media groups have been decided on and the argument as to space/time units and their frequency and reach has been settled we can get into the detail of choosing specific media. This is sometimes not open to very much choice – there is only one TV station or radio station that serves a particular region and often only one newspaper. With magazines and national newspapers the choice is wider and will usually be made on detailed study of the statistics and in the light of the prices that can be achieved through negotiation.

If you are aiming not at a large, national, consumer market but one which is local or regional or limited to members of a particular interest group, then your media choice will often be more limited and the accompanying information may be very scanty. Trade magazines, particularly, have tended to move into the 'controlled circulation' camp – in other words, they are sent unrequested to all people in a particular industry. Two different magazines may both approach the same industry, claim virtually the same circulation and cost much the same amount. The rate of response can however be alarmingly different. Obviously this is a function of the fact that sending somebody a magazine does not ensure that he reads it. If controlled circulation magazines are not interesting to the people who receive them then they are valueless to you.

Really the only way to test this factor is to try an ad with a coupon keyed to the magazine for response. Such response measurements are obviously appropriate in magazines but they can also be achieved in local newspapers and in local radio. The important thing is to keep your response figures carefully recorded and correlate them with the media cost. The sum is simple:

$$\frac{\text{cost of advertisement}}{\text{number of replies}} = \text{cost per reply}$$

This sum should be performed for each advertisement and can then form the basis of a number of different calculations as well as helping you choose the more effective publication. For instance, the cost per reply (CPR) can vary in the same magazine, in which case it suggests either that the time of year is less favourable or that the advertisement itself is less effective. If this system is carefully and consistently used then you will soon develop response 'norms' and discard advertisements that fail to meet them.

(A word of warning here. Measurements of cost per reply usually favour smaller advertisements. While this will hopefully help you resist the strong tendency towards graphic overkill that characterises some admen, it will hopefully not lead you to make all your ads overcrowded little, postage-stamp-sized entities. Even though they may work best under strictly economic measurements, they are unlikely to reflect credit and stature on your organisation.)

Given that you have the possibility of following the process through from the response to an ad to the final sale, then you can add another statistic:

$$\frac{\text{replies received}}{\text{sales achieved}} \times \text{CPR} = \text{cost per sale}$$

This assumes that you are selling something at a fixed price. However you may be in the position where sales values vary enormously. In this case you should simply compare the media cost of each advertisement with the sales volume achieved to get the net sales effectiveness:

sales value − media cost = net sales effectiveness.

Continuity vs 'bursts'

The final question the media planner must decide is whether to spend his money in a continuous stream or whether to split it into some bursts with dead periods in between. Once again, there are circumstances that favour one approach and other circumstances that favour the other. These are the factors that tend to encourage continuous advertising:

Frequent purchase pattern
High level of impulse buying
Expanding market
No budget constraints

And these are the factors that tend to encourage burst patterns of advertising:

Budget limitations
Infrequent purchase pattern
Heavy launch weight needed
Strong consumer loyalty to company brand.

The media plan

When all these factors have been considered the actual preparation of a media plan can be undertaken. In the media plan, the various points listed above are formally considered under the following headings:

1. *Media objectives*
Define the target audience in media terms and clarify what reach and frequency (ie what OTS) against that audience is desired. Objectives should also be qualified by other considerations such as the timing of the campaign, the regional weighting of it and other matters such as, for instance, a decision to increase media weight if competitors do so, thus maintaining a constant 'share of voice'.

2. *Limiting factors*

These are usually two, the creative requirements ie minimum size or time length that is needed to do justice to the ad, the need for colour etc, and the budget availability. There may be others. I remember a managing director who had such an animus against one newspaper that he refused to appear in it although it regularly came top of any independent evaluation of the papers that were suitable for his product.

3. *Media strategy*

In the light of the objectives and the factors mentioned above, evaluate all the media available and determine which are candidates and which fail to meet one or more of the requirements. Concentrate on the inter-media choice first, coming up with a simple strategic recommendation: eg 'We recommend TV as basis medium with some 60 per cent of the budget, adding a heavy poster campaign to add frequency and continuity of impression,' or 'We recommend using national newspapers as the basis medium, doubling the media weight via regional newspapers in those areas where potential is above average.'

4. *Media execution*

Having explained your fundamental strategy and demonstrated its soundness, then move to the question of the exact magazines, newspapers chosen – the intra-media choice. These choices can be simpler and easier to justify if a fundamental strategic approach is agreed first.

5. *The media plan*

This final section shows the actual costings and schedules – which ads appear where and what they cost.

The importance of negotiation

It is important to realise that media buying is a skilful and hard-nosed profession which can add a lot of value to the analytical skills of the media planner. The basic rules are:

- Assume media prices are negotiable. Always aim to get something off the price, even if it is only the three series rate for just two ads.

- Understand that media will only negotiate if there is something in it for them as well as for you. Putting the whole budget into one magazine where you would otherwise split it between two deadly rivals, can, for instance, be a way of achieving buying economies.
- Do not be tempted away from a sound strategy simply because of a cheap media buy. If a medium is wrong for your product, for your audience, for your campaign needs then it will not suddenly become right if it is cheaper.
- Maintain a tactical reserve within your plan for short-term buying. You can sometimes snap up ads at distress rates when somebody else has cancelled at the last minute. The media rapidly learn who can be expected to say yes quickly to a good deal and you will be offered such deals if you earn the reputation of being decisive. But do not be tempted away from your fundamental media strategy simply by bargains.

CHAPTER 20

Arousing Interest

I am very sceptical of these simplistic books about advertising that tell you the whole secret of the business lies in the formula AIDA – which is not as you might think the opera by Verdi, but a mnemonic that conceals the words

> ATTENTION
> INTEREST
> DESIRE
> ACTION.

This school suggest that these are the things that you have, in this order, to win from your audience.

In the formula itself there is nothing particularly harmful since some such series of gates must in truth be gone through if a sale is to be reached. People can hardly be persuaded to take the action of buying unless, first, some sort of wish to possess the product has been created. They can hardly feel that desire unless they have first been interested, and they can hardly be interested unless their attention has been gained. The problem with this formula is that, because it looks at the craft of ad-making as a series of steps, it often tends to produce ads that also reflect those steps. First they shout 'Stop!' or 'Look!' at you, attempting to gain your attention. They then bring in a headline which is supposed to arouse interest. This is followed by some copy directed towards the arousal of desire and the ad closes with a plea to 'Get some today'. Such advertisements do not achieve very much.

Effective advertisements do all the things these formula ads attempt to do – they attract attention, arouse interest, stimulate desire and produce action – but the difference is that they do it all at the same time. As to how they do it, we should perhaps look at the central issue of interest.

We have seen, when discussing communication, that relevance to the consumer's interests, desires and needs was key. People are self-centred and primarily are capable of interest only if the subject affects them. We have also made the observation that phoney interest is invariably detected as such. Generally you cannot trick people into being interested in something, and if you do succeed then their resentment is all the greater when they find out, as they inevitably must.

In fact – despite the distinction drawn by AIDA devotees – attracting attention and arousing interest are almost the same thing. At least they form a logical continuum, since the borrowed attention values (the bikini-clad girl in the ad for spark plugs) are known not to work. And the key to this desirable effect is to *discover the point where the product's advantages and the relevant self-interest of the reader overlap.*

Now, if we have done our work well, if we have developed a clear product positioning, for instance, and if we have progressed this into a copy strategy which is capable of working, then we should not find it too difficult to discover what it is that brings product and reader (or viewer) together. All our developmental work on strategy says 'Look at this problem from the consumer's point of view. Find out what the consumer wants. Find out what is in your product that can help him fill that want.' If we have done this well, then we should be focused on the consumer and understand his needs and understand our product in terms of his needs – so finding that point should not require a lot of study.

It is important to realise that attention and interest are given to advertisements in vastly differing quantities. Reading and noting studies are conducted in major magazines – they show attention for full-colour, full-page ads varying between 20 per cent of the readers of the publication to 80 per cent. Recall studies are carried out on TV commercials – viewers are asked what commercials they remember from their last evening's viewing. Prompted memory of commercials of the same length also shows much the same sort of spread – 20 per cent to 80 per cent.

Such statistics give a crude warning of how vital copy is. The best media buyer in the world cannot buy so efficiently that he can make up more than a tiny percentage of the money that an inadequate copywriter can squander. Sometimes, of course, low-scoring ads are produced by the fact that the goods advertised are only of interest to a small minority of the readers or viewers concerned. In these cases, if you attract the attention of every one of these people, then you can well afford to let the others go hang. However we also see such disparities in score between ads for products that logically have the same broad appeal and the same potential audience. Here it simply means you are getting only 20p or 30p or whatever it is for every £1 you invest.

We can be quite clear that a lot of ads that score poorly in terms of attention and interest do so because of obvious mistakes that would be eliminated by sensible strategic planning earlier. Such mistakes are:

1. *No clear promise.* The secret of attention is to show the reader how the product will affect him. If no clear product promise has been isolated, then it will hardly appear in the ad. So why should the reader be interested?

2. *'We orientation'.* A good copy strategy will scotch a campaign that is 'we oriented', that talks about what we the company have done, rather than what you the consumer can expect. If such thinking survives to the printed page or to the TV screen then it will always result in poor scores.

3. *Borrowed interest.* We have seen that borrowed interest is usually rapidly seen for what it is. It is far less likely to be resorted to, if the trouble has been taken to develop a strong and unique story for the product.

4. *Common Positioning.* All too often brands develop positionings which are not unique but common in the market. These are then reflected in selling ideas which are generic. It is not very easy, against such a background, to develop advertisements that are unique and different and arresting.

5. *Wrong target audience.* This is a particularly insidious danger and it affects even those companies that have a mass of research behind them. One measures the attention given to the advertising and, because the raw percentages are reasonable, does not enquire into their composition. It may well be that a false campaign is attracting the attention of people who are not members of your target audience, while your true, predestined customers are ignoring you.

These are the maladies that are likely to show themselves in poor attention values. In these cases, the poor attention and interest is only a symptom. The real problem lies deeper.

But we still find great differences in interest level between ads that are impeccably on strategy and where none of these problems listed above apply. Are there any techniques that can be used here?

The central principle is perhaps to forget 'attention' and 'interest' –

they only lead to headlines that shout 'Look!' and automatically evoke the response, 'Why the hell should I look?' – and consider what you are actually trying to do. You are trying to involve your reader. Here are four fundamental ways to get involvement. They are used all the time in ads and commercials that win high attention.

1. *Seek a new slant on the familiar.* Sometimes you are in the happy position of having a product which is genuinely and sensationally new. All too often you have a product which has little real novelty and whose superiority or difference is fairly marginal. (This is hardly suprising – technology inches forward rather than taking massive leaps.) Explore your product however and you will probably find a way of presenting some sort of new slant on it, even if it does in fact do pretty much what competitors have done for a long time.

An award-winning ad for Nulon hand cream years ago showed a large picture of a woman's hands under water and used the headline: 'Picture of a lady *drying* her hands'. Hand-care was not new and Nulon did more or less what other hand lotions did. But the effect of presenting the apparent contradiction, that wetting your hands actually dried them, was a novel, involving suggestion. Note too that it was not by any means unfamiliar. The people who read the ad recognised at once what it was saying. It fitted in to their established pattern of things but still had the benefit of some surprise and some novelty.

This technique requires some considerable care. If the approach is too *outré* then it will be rejected or not understood which means it will simply be ignored. A very fine sense of balance is required.

Similar in effect is the Toyota ad earlier that referred to twin valves per cylinder as 'an extra pair of lungs' – it explains a technical feature in anthropological terms that make it illuminating and understandable.

2. *Seek emotional involvement.* Because products fulfil human needs there are often legitimate emotional reasons for buying them. The acceptable level of emotion, and the way it is expressed, varies however from product category to product category, medium to medium, audience to audience. It is most noticeable when we compare the much broader use of emotion in American advertising with that used in Britain. Kodak, for instance, has run commercials for many years in America that position a family's record in its photographs as a highly charged matter. Such commercials make

121

British audiences uncomfortable – at least, they seem to when they are shown in large-scale screenings to young, cynical advertising professionals. Whether they would have this effect in the greater intimacy of television addressed to the intended audience of parents is another matter. My personal feeling is that we are often unnecessarily cautious of an emotional content in our campaigns and neglect its massive involving power. Once again a skilful, sensitive touch is required – Fairy Liquid managed such a touch for years – and in Britain it may be necessary to exorcise the emotional with a final smile.

3. *Use the disarming effect of humour*. Advertising in Britain has always made much use of humour and there are certainly good reasons for it, as well as some very bad results. That it can involve in all sorts of ways is clear. It can also be a massive irrelevance. Since humour is such a difficult subject we have an entire chapter on the subject further on.

4. *Encourage the reader to discover something*. We have already commented on the knowledge – a commonplace of learning theory for many decades – that retention is improved if the new knowledge has been acquired by personal experience rather than by teaching. The moral is to encourage the reader (or viewer or listener, these words are always interchangeable) to find out for himself the message you wish to communicate. Asking questions can be a potent force in self-discovery, as the classic ad for the Sherwin Cody School of English shows. Making comparisons – always an effective technique – and then inviting the reader to draw his own conclusions can also be very effective. *Reader's Digest* has used self-evaluation quizzes and tests as part of its editorial for years, as do a lot of popular women's magazines. These are exercises in self-discovery and they enable us to find out more about the most fascinating subject in the world – ME.

5. *Exploit related interest*. I am a little frightened to mention this one at all after inveighing so vehemently against borrowed interest. But there is interest which is not totally germane yet so related that it can be used without leading to the attraction of the wrong audience and the inevitable switch-off. Personalities used as spokesmen are a good example of what can be borrowed interest. The person may have little relevance or apparent competence, but when the right person is recruited and seen by the audience as competent and relevant he or she can add a lot of strength to your ad. The use of René Cutforth by

Figure 20 Self-evaluation quizzes are high on interest – used here to recruit Army officers

Krona was an example of a spokesman who added documentary strength to a story simply because he was quite different from the polished, polite media figure who usually presents food ads.

A commercial for Ariel uses the testimonial of a lady whose business is the rental of wedding dresses. This also borders on borrowed interest but is saved by the fact that the setting is familiar and the step from this field to the everyday is only small.

Every single one of these ways of increasing attention and interest carries, like a packet of cigarettes, a caution written on it. Increasing attention and interest is skilful, delicate work. It requires a fine touch. Yet most breakthroughs in this area of advertising come from going that tiny half step further than anybody has dared do before. One is constantly asking onself, 'What if we did so-and-so?'

A useful discipline is not simply to take the first solution that is offered but to look at this solution, saying 'Can we step back a half pace and would it still work?' or 'We have taken one step here. What happens if we take two?' The point is that the very successful campaigns are only slightly different to the run-of-the-mill campaigns – only slightly different in everything but their results, that is.

CHAPTER 21

Achieving Conviction

We live in a world where large-scale advertising has been a fact of life for many years and it is reasonable to believe that many people are not totally naive about the validity of advertising claims. Many have grown up with a healthy scepticism.

The work of the Advertising Standards Authority is worthy and valuable, but most people, I imagine, think that advertisers have little if any control on their truthfulness. One does not expect advertisements to lie directly – but one recognises that they are a form of special pleading that accentuates the positive and seeks to eliminate the negative. This cautious reserve is something the advertiser must learn to live with. He must also find ways of combating it. After all, he wishes his advertisements to produce belief and, consequent upon that belief, action.

It is as well to realise that conviction, just like attention and just like interest, is not something that exists in a vacuum. Neither is conviction something one can address oneself to after one has attracted attention and aroused interest. One cannot say, 'Now I am going to convince you of the truth of what I have been saying,' and hope that it will work. Conviction must be the inescapable result of the entire advertisement.

People react to advertisements in very much the same sort of instinctive way we adopt when dealing with people. Truthfulness and honesty are qualities we make projective judgements about. They are the result of your assessment of the total personality.

This said, however, there clearly are ways that people can increase their credibility; guarantees they can offer, evidence and testimonials from reliable sources and so on. Advertising campaigns can use the same methods to achieve the same results.

Conviction is a quality that all advertising seeks to produce, but it is much more important for some products than others and for some types of product claims than others.

Generally, conviction is an important element:

- In product categories that are comparatively high-priced.
- Where there are a number of similar products and the differences between them are known to be small.
- Where the product performance is not readily verifiable by the purchaser.
- Where a specific, measurable type of performance is desired.
- Where the campaign is attempting to communicate a significantly better type of performance than this category has traditionally delivered.
- Where the standing and probity of the company behind the product is an important element – for instance, in the financial field.

Conviction is much less important:

- In low-cost impulse goods.
- Where the product performance is immediate and obvious.
- Where the product performance is essentially subjective.

It will be seen from the above that conviction is an important factor in most functional goods and high-ticket items. It can also be very important even in other areas if the performance is not readily verifiable. One expects a chocolate bar to claim that it is delicious and realises this is in the final analysis a matter of opinion, but one requires much more solid evidence if one is to believe that the same chocolate bar is less likely to cause tooth decay.

Precisely the cases where conviction is important are the cases where scepticism is most widespread. So the more we need to be believed, the harder it may be to achieve.

What are the techniques we can use to gain belief?

1. Be specific

One of the oldest advertising claims in the world is Ivory Soap's '99 and 44/100ths pure'. That pernickety fraction is a lot more convincing than any blanket 100 per cent – it makes you think somebody may have actually measured it.

Specific numbers are inherently believable. So are specific names – don't say 'used by some of the biggest companies', say 'used by ICI, Ford, Thorn EMI, Shell and Esso'. Specific ingredients are believable. Specific addresses are believable. Specific details of technical processes are believable.

A word of warning here. Many advertisers are frightened of the specific. They assume because they list five of the single malt whiskies they put in their blend this year that people will hold it against them if they use two different ones next year.

They also counter questions about technical processes by saying, 'Oh, there's nothing special about what we do, everybody does much the same.'

This is to misunderstand the effect of the specific. It is not that the hard-pressed consumer wants to remember all the detail you give him. It is not that he will research the data you provide to find out if it really is unique. Being specific works because of the willingness you display towards disclosing details. It says, in effect, 'We have nothing to hide.' It commands trust and respect.

2. Understate

Since scepticism about advertising has become so widespread it is often more effective to understate a superiority. You doubt it?

Consider those claims one sees all the time in the 'up to' form. 'Saves up to 38 per cent of fuel', 'Gives you up to 27 per cent more mileage'.

The 'up to' is there because the figures can, in all honesty, vary and the advertiser wants to quote the best figure he can but realises that it won't always be achieved. But what does that 'up to' communicate? It communicates surely that the quoted figure is as good as unattainable in most ordinary circumstances and that I can expect to get a good deal less. Suppose then, instead of saying 'up to 27 per cent more mileage' I say 'at least 12 per cent more mileage – some have got much more'. Is today's consumer, bred on ITV in his cradle, likely to be less impressed?

It may often be a good idea to junk these universal percentages that I suspect creep into copy simply because of a desire to use big numbers, and try to say the same thing in a harder, clearer way – 'gives you at least 12 miles where you only got 10 before'. Believability is a matter of some very subtle nuances.

3. Demonstrate

Books like this one are constantly lauding the demonstration power of TV. Yet how often is this power ignored? How often do you see a product which cries out for demonstration using flat, generic advertising?

Demonstration is powerful and should be more used. The fact that it is used so little is another reason to use it more. Also demonstration should be used more *imaginatively*. Because filmed demonstrations are troublesome and difficult to film and because they don't seem to give anybody much of a reputation for being 'creative', they either don't get used at all or are scamped and carried through with little thought or care. Think about demonstration sequences and lavish care on them to make them more effective. (We shall have some specific suggestions in our TV chapter.)

4. Explain how it works

Demonstration is one very effective way of explaining how a product does what we say it does. It is certainly not the only one. It can be done, for instance, by analogy – Gillette had a powerful commercial for their TracII razor that used the analogy of a twin snow plough. It can be done by explaining in simple words alone. Usually, by explaining processes that other advertisers skip over, you will communicate a transparent honesty that will aid conviction.

5. Use independent testimony

The innate doubt that people have about advertisements springs from the simple fact that advertisements are avowedly partial. They are paid for by the advertiser and have the aim of bringing you round to their way of thinking. An obvious way to counteract this factor is to use independent testimony in some form if it is available or can be made available.

Independent authority can be used in advertisements in many ways. At the very simplest levels, your product possibly meets a British Standard. There is no harm in saying so. Your lemonade or toilet paper may be no better then anybody else's but if your customers number the Savoy Hotel and Pan American Airways, then mentioning the fact can possibly mark yours off as superior to the rest.

The use of the man and woman in the street – or in the supermarket or the pub or wherever your product takes them – can do a lot for credibility. In broadcast media there is an immediate and totally different sound to ordinary unscripted speech which automatically communicates genuineness and unbribeability.

In print media this radically different sound does not apply – but the enthusiastic letters you get from your customers are equally obviously genuine. In certain fields, there is absolutely no lack of rave notices, simply because there is so much written – even if a new car is very widely panned there will be enough positive quotes from motoring journalists to fill a sizeable campaign.

CHAPTER 22

Wholeness

The trouble with books like this is that they convey the message that effective advertising – or any kind of effective communication – can be produced on the aggregative principle. You decide on your basic message, you formulate a claim, then you add some support for the claim, then you decide on an arresting picture, add to that an interesting headline, and then write some body copy that is informative and ends with an appeal for action. Do all that and – so the books seem to say – you will have a perfect advertisement.

What you will actually have is an ill-assorted collection of bits that probably look as unlikely and unrelated as they in fact are. You will have a monster reminiscent of the camel that was described – rather unfairly – as a horse designed by a committee.

I suggest you go back in your mind over campaigns that you can remember – and how alarmingly few they are compared to the thousands of ads confronting us every day! They, you will find, are not like that. They are often all of them very different from each other, suggesting that the one right way to do it is illusory. But what they for the most part do have in common is an *identifiable, central idea which informs all the parts*.

Let us look at a few such campaigns.

Courvoisier seems to me much the most effectively advertised brand of Cognac. The reason is a very valuable central idea – the brandy of Napoleon. Whatever we British may think of Napoleon, he seems to have a unique position as a brandy drinker (not, I believe, in any way justified by his essentially rather frugal habits). Courvoisier have the Imperial shadow emerging behind the bottle in every ad and cropping up on every showcard. The little Corsican is on the bottle itself, of course. He is also likely to turn up on any promotional material.

'The Brandy of Napoleon' is a strong claim because it contains a number of ingredients – it suggests age, which rightly or wrongly is given almost mystic credit for excellence in the brandy-drinker's mind. It also

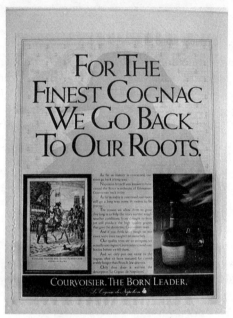

Figure 21   Courvoisier – making the most of Napoleon

is very clearly French. It is masculine – and that seems to be an important dimension for spirits. It suggests quality – if the Emperor could not afford the best, who could?

The important thing about this campaign is that the central idea is a *unifying element*. Once this selling idea has been adopted then the visual elements of the ads, their copy content, the images on showcards, the style of promotions chosen, these all fall into place more or less automatically. The campaign inevitably has that characteristic which is hardest to achieve but in the last analysis perhaps is most vital – *wholeness*.

Wholeness is so important because the human mind cannot store and remember and relate a whole lot of trivial, disparate things. It is only when the things we have to remember form logical, integrated clusters in the mind that we can remember them. This applies in relation to those things that we urgently need to remember – details of our work, of our family lives, of our hobbies and enthusiasms. How much more likely is such a rule to apply to those hundreds of commercial products that compete for our attention?

Marlboro is another outstanding example of a product that has a unique and uniformly informing central idea. Cowboys, Western

130

scenery, the great outdoors – these elements go through everything the brand does (at least, where the regulations allow it) and communicate much of what the brand wishes to communicate.

Just as in Courvoisier's harnessing of Napoleon, the cowboy imagery communicates much of what Marlboro wishes to communicate. The primary imagery is very masculine – Marlboro cowboys don't tote guns but who doubts that they are real men? It also has the clean, healthy components implicit in the wide skies, the bare rocks, the empty range. The imagery is also nostalgic and reminiscent of a world where the present-day worry about smoking did not exist.

Saab has found a similar, simple, profiling idea in the fact that the company also makes aircraft. Applied to a car, this idea suggests that they will have technical standards almost automatically more demanding and more advanced than other car manufacturers.

It is an idea, once found, that again informs all communicative activity. It means that aircraft and aeronautical symbols play a major visual role in all ads and brochures. It imparts a constant accent to all copy.

Perrier has found a very simple way to set itself off from all other mineral waters, by stealing the French word for water: 'eau'.

This monosyllabic idea contains a lot. It makes Perrier the archetypal mineral water. It makes them the only really French mineral water. And it communicates a subtle chic which nobody else can take. No wonder they lead the rapidly expanding market!

Now, ideas of this kind that stem from the product's fundamental positioning and can be utilised over the entire spectrum of advertising communication are light-years away from so-called creative ideas that have no real relation to the positioning. There are lots of these about too. I can only presume they are there because they are sometimes fun. They do nothing else.

Harvey's Bristol Cream has elected to show itself as consumed by Attila the Hun and his wife. Why? Sherry has nothing to do with the barbarian hordes from the East. It does not communicate any of the ideas that the product could legitimately wish to communicate – proud, seafaring Bristol merchants, the sun-ripened grapes of Spain, skilled blenders in Jerez, the long tradition of *oloroso* sherries as part of the secure, prosperous Victorian age, the place of sweet, comforting drinks at Christmas. All these are valid ideas. This idea is simply 'a nice idea for a commercial' and one that incidentally shows, with the precision of every Freudian slip, exactly what the copywriter thinks of the masses who buy his product at Christmas in the supermarkets!

> *Shredded Wheat* chooses to tell its story by potted, presumably amusing commercials culled from the backwoods of American history. Now, British TV viewers are not particularly tolerant of their own history – and are certainly bored to uncomprehending desperation by somebody else's. The product has been in Britain since the beginning of the century so it certainly has no American background to apologise for. Another example of an idea which does nothing for the product it is supposed to serve.

The moral from all this is that, just because there is undeniably an idea there, it is not necessarily a good one and more often than not, it is not one of those great, all-encompassing ideas that go on for years and are at the heart of very successful long-lived campaigns and long-lived brands.

How can one find such ideas, and how can one be sure that one has such an idea when it is found?

1. *Always work from the product outwards.* Start your search from the standpoint of the product and its positioning. Too many advertisements are developed the other way around – copywriters want to shoot a parody of *The Great Gatsby* and look for a product that might be prepared to pick up the tab. This cannot happen if you never take your eyes off the product.

2. *Be aware of the true, legitimate worth of the product.* Because the products we work for come in gaudy boxes and sit on the shelves of the supermarket we assume they are dull. They are not. Find the real glamour and excitement in the product if it is glamour and excitement you want.

3. *Be sure the idea is large enough to last for years.* If it is an admittedly clever play on words, or a one-off visual, then it is probably not the big idea that will keep the product going for years. A really good idea should immediately suggest a dozen totally different executions. If it can only be done one way it will become a straitjacket very quickly.

4. *Be sure the idea communicates what you want it to communicate.* Examine every idea coldly and analytically. If it communicates something different from what you want it to communicate, then junk it.

5. *Hold on to good ideas and don't lose them for inadequate reasons.* There are undoubtedly great advertising ideas of the past that lived on beyond their usefulness. But there were certainly many more that got changed just because a certain ennui had crept in at the company or the agency.

Rosser Reeves expresses the problem with typical force when he says: 'a new management brings crashing to the earth one of the giants of the forest, apparently for no other reason than a desire to rearrange the advertising landscape'. A good idea is inevitably a very rare thing. Do not assume that there are a dozen others just as good because one may not appeal to you. If you have a good one hold fast to it.

PART FOUR

The Individual Advertisement

CHAPTER 23

The Most Important Words in the Ad – Effective Headlines and Claims

When you are writing a press advertisement (the rules for film are somewhat different) the decision on the headline is the most important single decision in the ad.

Usually the headline is the idea of the ad in its most elementary form. We refer to ads by their headlines, just as we refer to books by their titles. Headlines dictate what follows – define which pictures are to be used, which arguments are to be employed and with what emphasis.

(There are, of course, ads without headlines, that just charge straight into the body copy. The readership levels for such ads are almost always catastrophic. While I am innately conservative about saying 'never' to any creative solution in advertising I am strongly inclined to be this categoric about headline-less ads.)

So what are the points to remember in writing effective headlines?

1. How much to tell – how much to conceal?

A central dilemma is often posed by the fact that a good headline must perform two apparently contradictory functions. It must tell enough to let you get the fundamentals of what the product is offering, yet it should also arouse your interest and curiosity and make you want to know more.

(There is a small school of advertising people, invincibly removed from reality, who look at headlines simply in terms of doing the second of these two jobs. The more impenetrable and incomprehensible the better, in their book. 'If they can't understand, then we *force* them to read the copy,' goes the theory. Sadly, in this democratic age, any attempts to force readers to do anything are doomed to failure. The world is full of things that I am rather glad not to have to bother with and incomprehensible advertisements come high on this list.)

Advertisers whose products enjoy fairly low interest and whose market consists of virtually everybody – impulse products, functional products – often take the opposite view that picture and headline must communicate the full story, that the body copy is there strictly as a back-up for those who want it. Even within this situation it is possible to write headlines that have a little more intrigue and interest than simple transliterations of the copy strategy. Such ads often employ headlines which are not strictly headlines in the sense of aiming to encourage further reading. They are often *claims* – a summary of the copy strategy and its main promise, probably used over and over again. We shall have a look at claims a little later.

2. Are there any 'magic' words?

Much of the advice to copywriters on headline-writing points out that there are a number of words that recur frequently in headlines of proven effectiveness. Such words are NEW, PRESENTING, ANNOUNCING, NOW, IMPORTANT DEVELOPMENT, STARTLING, QUICK, EASY, ADVICE TO, HOW TO, WHY, THE TRUTH ABOUT … It is rather naive to think that the effectiveness of these headlines comes from these specific words. Effectiveness comes primarily from content and only secondarily from the exact words used. There is a strong interest in products that are new and better and understandably such products tend to be advertised with headlines that use words like NEW, PRESENTING and so on. If you have something new and sensational to advertise then do, by all means, use words like these in the headline. They are not – as some people maintain – hackneyed and tired. Newness and innovation are still interesting and always will be, but it is the newness and innovation which attract attention rather than the specific words.

The case of HOW TO and WHY is a little different. Headlines that begin with these words invite further reading. Attention and that further reading are, of course, crucially dependent on what exactly one is offered instruction in. HOW TO MAKE 1 MILLION A YEAR is a headline that many people, for understandable reasons, will grant a second glance.

HOW TO GET A DEGREE IN ANCIENT HEBREW is of considerably more limited interest. WHY DARK-HAIRED MEN LIVE LONGER is of wide interest to both dark and fair, WHY ACCOUNTANCY IS NOT BORING (to steal a delightful title from the Monty Python people) promises to make anyone but accountants yawn.

3. How long should headlines be?

It may surprise you to learn that a mass of research has proved nothing against the long headline. Reading and noting studies show no difference in attention values that are related to headline length. Mail order advertisers, the effectiveness of whose ads can be measured very precisely, tend to get poor results from very short headlines (just one or two words) but they get more or less the same values for headlines with up to 12 words and for headlines with up to 24 words. Once again one should try to look behind the figures and understand *why*.

Only a very simple (and frequently that means a very obvious and banal) thought can be expressed in a couple of words. Thoughts which are so fascinating that they make you want to read on usually need more words. They may need quite a lot of words – if the fascination is there, the words will be read.

Writing a headline, you are trying to provoke two somewhat different reactions. One is the reaction, 'Mmm! That's what I want to know. Let's find out more about it.' The other is the reaction, 'Just a moment, there's something there that doesn't gel. I'll have to find out about it.' That this complexity of reaction is more easily achieved with a headline that is a fair-sized sentence in its own right is almost inevitable. It is often effective to make the clear, valid product promise – and then add a comment that increases curiosity and the desire to find out more. That is the technique of Claude Hopkins' Pepsodent campaign: FILM – THE ROBBER OF ALL TOOTH BEAUTY. LEARN HOW MILLIONS NOW COMBAT IT.

4. Be specific – use facts and numbers

All copy is strengthened by being specific and headlines respond magnificently to it. David Ogilvy's famous Rolls Royce headline is an excellent example: 'AT 60 MILES AN HOUR THE LOUDEST NOISE IN THIS NEW ROLLS-ROYCE COMES FROM THE ELECTRIC CLOCK'. Numbers are more effective in headlines than the same thing in words ('4' instead of 'four'). They communicate more quickly and they save space. Using numbers can make a three-line headline a two-liner!

5. Effective headlines are addressed to the reader

Again this seems obvious. If you are aiming to get the reader to read, then phrase the headline in terms that make clear its relevance to him. But how many headlines do you see that tell you what 'we' (the company) do and apparently have nothing to offer you?

Good headlines don't just use the word 'you', they actually select the desired reader and force him to read. Here's a nice example from Olympus: 'YOU MAY BE AN AMATEUR PHOTOGRAPHER BUT YOU'LL NEVER TAKE ANOTHER AMATEUR PHOTOGRAPH.' Not only is it a strong promise, it selects very clearly the amateur photographer who has the ambition to take better photographs. Why the quotes? This ad is also a testimonial from David Bailey so the promise gets an extra dimension of believability from this source.

6. What about puns and word play?

Most people don't need any encouragement to use 'clever' word plays in ads, and all too often they are a dangerous indulgence.

But if they really work – if they don't impair understanding but give it some kind of extra dimension – then they can be very helpful. Here is a

Figure 22 Olympus – good headline and use of testimonial

headline with which the Army seeks to lure school leavers away from the business career they might probably choose and in the direction of the Queen's shilling. The illustration shows a young officer in charge of a tank on a country road: A COMPANY CAR BY THE TIME YOU'RE 21 (AND A COMPANY BY 28). Ford has a piece of word play which works in the headline: CAN YOU B B B BBBBBBBBBBBBBRAKE 15 TIMES A SECOND? A neat way to refer to the new kind of brakes that come on and off for infinitesimal periods to stop them blocking and skidding.

Both these examples show the two most important factors in using such devices in headlines:

    a.   The wordplay does not impede understanding but in fact aids it.
    b.   The wordplay directs attention at the key part of the strategy and not at an irrelevance.

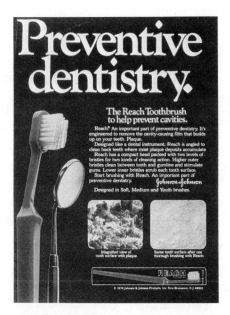 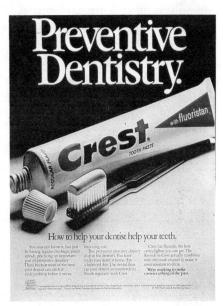

Figure 23 The trouble with bright, short, snappy lines is that two people can have the same idea simultaneously

7. Headline and illustration should work together

Effective headlines often modify and are modified by the illustration – headline and picture work together to communicate *one* idea. Ads like this can be very crisp and quick. Like the Honda Motorcycle ad that simply showed the product with an eager aficionado riding it and added the two words: MEN'S LIB. Or the ad that laid out neat rows of fruit-flavoured Lifesavers and the injunction: PLEASE DO NOT LICK THIS PAGE. I have already mentioned the Nulon advertisement where the illustration of hands under water was balanced by the apparently contradictory headline: PICTURE OF A LADY *DRYING* HER HANDS.

8. The special case of the claim

It could of course be argued that the claim constitutes the most important words in an advertisement, since it is the summary of what you wish to communicate and will be used in all probability over a long period whereas headlines are usually used for one ad only.

Claims have a different function, of course. They do not aim to encourage people to read on, they are a summary – and hopefully a memorable one. Effective claims have some characteristics of their own:

They are on strategy. Obviously they are, since they are the summation of that strategy. However, you would be surprised how often people suggest claims which are a clever summation of the execution, rather than a summary of the product's promise. A good claim should be usable on any execution.

They are competitive. They express the product's promise in a way that makes it seem either superior to others or unique. They do not express it as generic. This does not necessarily mean using comparatives. In fact, claims which use comparatives are often weak because they have little uniqueness and little distinction. 'Now hands that do dishes can feel soft as your face' had a strong competitive edge, but expressed it in a way that was distinctive and timeless.

They do not run the risk of being outdated. A claim based on a superiority which will probably prove to be short-lived is not a good investment.

They make you think about the product. A good claim will give you a flash of insight and understanding about a product. While this may be a new piece of factual information, it can equally well be a way of looking at facts which are well enough known. The Greek Tourist Office in the US ran a claim which I always found very strong and relevant for any member of Western society – YOU WERE BORN IN GREECE. There is no new information there, but suddenly a very real and urgent reason to get to know this country and to distinguish it from other places that also have ruins and sun.

CHAPTER 24

How to Use Words Well – Ways to Effective Body Copy

Finally, someone has to get out the whole ad.

Whereas the great copywriters of the 1920s and 1930s started work at this point, pitting their wits and their feel for the consumer against a piece of white paper, this is, for us, a comparatively late stage in the development of a campaign. This fact should not blind us to its importance.

All the various forms of intellectual work that have occupied us up to this stage have simply been preparations for that point when an actual advertisement has to be conceived and written.

Notice I say written. Ads – even TV commercials – are *written*. Until someone takes the trouble to put them on paper, word for word, from beginning to end, they are really nothing more than vague ideas that may or may not be of value. Today we have a new race of vocal, intelligent art directors, used to thinking in terms of advertising ideas, and the vogue is for ads to be conceived by writers and art directors working together. I certainly do not decry this system – which is undoubtedly better than the old one where a copywriter would write an ad in complete detail and then take it along to somebody who would pull a layout together, with almost no thought for its content. But the new system seems to require a senior partner and a junior partner and, in my experience, the senior partner is usually the copywriter. Words come first in the business of persuasion. There is no fundamental reason why they have to – but they almost always do.

It is also true that, however much we may praise teamwork, writing is a lonely business. Groups cannot write ads – all they can do is put together a confused hotch-potch of ideas that, when one takes the trouble to examine them closely, are often mutually exclusive. Persuasion is a one-to-one business and good copywriters treat it this way. They write with a clear idea of the person they wish to influence in their minds and they weigh every word till they have a complete, rounded selling message.

The way ads are conceived today (and I shall be talking in this chapter primarily of press advertisements; TV and radio have, to a certain extent, their own rules that we shall cover later) often tends to diminish the writer's role. First, the concentration on positioning and strategy can easily make writing seem less important than it is. Second, the way campaigns are presented, sold and bought often works against it. Typically a wall full of layouts is studied by a large and disparate group that draws its conclusions from the hardly natural reading distance of ten or twelve feet. Some ads are bought and others rejected – not unreasonably – on the appeal of headline and picture. The ones that get bought get 'progressed' – and at that stage an often junior writer is brought in to fill in the body copy.

The emphasis on headline and picture is certainly not wrong. These are the elements that decide the ad's success. But the cavalier treatment of the copy is certainly not justified either. Consider that while it may well be true that four or five times as many people will read the headline as read the whole ad, those who do go right through are most likely to be the true prospects, they are certainly the most interested and they are the ones we have a real opportunity to sell something to. Advertising is too expensive to afford any second-class, second-quality persuasion.

The practice of regarding highly-paid creative directors as too good for body copy, and young copywriters as not good enough for headlines and concepts, does not work towards optimal advertising. Logically, the same person should frame the headline that attracts the reader in and then develop the whole sale that results from it. Writers who simply add the less important bits to other people's work are unlikely to do it with much love, care and conviction. And, similarly, creative directors who get used to conducting the orchestra but neglect their individual instruments, run the risk of losing their virtuoso skills.

There is a bitter joke in the agency world that says, whenever an ad is produced which is a miserable, uninspired hotch-potch, 'Ah, but you should have seen the copy strategy!'

The public we wish to influence only sees the finished ads. They are not party to the ingenious positioning statement, the carefully-filed and balanced copy strategy, the daring rough, the brilliant sales pitch from the creative director. All they know is what appears on the page. There, copy is king.

There are all sorts of little tips and hints that can improve copy. Many of them are no more than tips for good writing – and I cannot stress enough that a good copywriter must, first and foremost, be a good *writer*. He must like communicating with the written word and take the discipline of writing seriously. He must examine and re-examine every sentence, testing each word to see if he can make it harder, sharper and more real. He must be on constant guard against imprecision and muzziness and cliches. He must be sure of involving and interesting his readers in every sentence.

The advertising writer needs, to a significant degree more than most other writers, the negative capability that Keats praises. It is necessarily a very self-effacing kind of writing with one eye fixed firmly on the product and the other even more firmly on the prospective consumer. If there is one golden rule it is: *Be sure every word is relevant to the reader and is understood by the reader.*

You could write a book on copy alone. (One of the very best writers, Hanley Norins, has written one. It is called *The Compleat Copywriter* and is most earnestly recommended to all advertising writers.) In this chapter we can only cover some of the more important techniques and principles of copywriting.

Don't fall for the long copy/short copy gambit

People talk about long copy ads as though they are a special and unusual genus with its own rules. This is a deceptive way of looking at the matter. You should always write the amount of copy that you need to do a convincing selling job. This will often be quite little if it is a well-known product whose use is familiar and whose differences from its competitors are modest. If the product is a new one with many technical advantages, then very likely the copy will need to be longer. The sort of copy that is often described as 'long' usually fills half to three quarters of an A4 page and has about a quarter as many words as those perfectly-shaped, not-a-word-wasted little masterpieces by Maupassant – so the idea of 'long' is, to say the least, relative. Your copy should be the length it needs to be – not longer and not shorter.

Plan your total sales pitch

As you plan the ad, plan your copy as a salesman plans his sales pitch. Think in terms of paragraphs and know which argument follows which and how the whole thing is constructed.

It is well to be realistic and realise that only half the readers you attract into the copy will actually emerge at the other end. Make sure you have ways of keeping their attention and interest, and make sure that those who stop halfway through have still had the guts of the sale.

A well-constructed ad will usually follow a form much like this:

Paragraph 1 states the central theme of the sale in words that follow on logically from the headline. All the essentials have been stated, even if the reader gets no farther.

Paragraph 2 reverts to the reader's need for the product and his interests.

Paragraph 3 explains *how* the product can fulfil these needs in greater detail than has been possible before.

Paragraph 4 brings in subsidiary arguments, testimonials from satisfied users, specialised product uses, additional benefits etc.

Paragraph 5 sums up the main bones of the sale, urges prompt and specific action.

Every piece of copy will vary, simply because the priorities are different, but some sort of clear plan of this kind will make it easier to do the job well. It also makes it easier to defend the copy if you have given thought to the structure of the argument, not simply let it gather on the page.

Use every stylistic trick to hold attention

If copy is any longer than two or three sentences, then it is always wise to consider the use of subheads. Partially, these are a purely defensive measure. If you have a headline and four subheads following that, read consecutively, tell the bones of the story, then you have done your job even if the intermediate copy is unread.

However the subheads contribute more than a simple precis for lazy readers. They do quite demonstrably aid reading by providing the reader with convenient pauses and holding out a carrot to him to reach the next paragraph.

Essentially the same is true of any other devices that break up a forbidding grey mass of type. Frequent paragraphing does it, since it introduces white space and short lines. Little boxes with summaries, checklists, statistics or what have you do it. Suddenly putting a whole paragraph in bold type or in italics does it – presuming it is not totally unmotivated. Direct speech in quotation marks does it. And small illustrations help greatly – the captions to illustrations are second only to the headline of an ad in terms of the reading they attract. Why, oh why do we see so many illustrations without captions?

The reasons for all this are very simple. As Alice said, 'What's the use of a book without pictures or conversations?' All these devices have come to be associated with particularly interesting parts of a story by the editors whose typesetting habits have had such a strong influence on our reading habits. We respond to such stimuli.

Seek constantly for touches that add conviction

Since scepticism and disbelief is a fate that faces many ads, a good copywriter is always on the alert for little things that will add conviction. There are many of these.

When you name the price of a high-priced item, always put it in some sort of relationship to the value it offers – if you only use it four times a year it pays for itself, it's only risen by five per cent in the last 20 years, it only works out to so much a day, it can change your life yet costs no more than a meal for two at a good restaurant, it will appreciate in value, others are twice as much. If the price is low tell us why – we cut down on overheads in some way, we bought some bargain stock, this is a special introductory offer for a few buyers.

Independent enthusiasm and recommendation does not have to be the full-blown testimonial. A subordinate clause can list some of your big, well-known customers. Or mention the verdict of some independent testing unit. Or simply relate how many you have sold in the last year.

Make buying easy

Coupons make replying easy and should be included if this type of response is sought. But there are all sorts of other ways in which buying can be made easier. For instance, tell them the names of major chains and department stores that handle the product. Tell them how to get to a hard-to-find outlet. (Even little maps can be useful here. If the place is hard to find it can be a major hindrance to sales. Overcome it!) Give them solid reasons why they should buy *now*. You only have so many left. The prices will go up after the Budget. If you want people to respond by telephone give them the name of somebody to ask for – this, by the way, can make a quite excellent keying device to judge the response from various media. If they need to measure their living rooms or their children or themselves for the product in some way, tell them how to do it.

CHAPTER 25

A Place for Humour

Claude Hopkins, the first advertising guru, is absolute.

'People do not buy from clowns.'

Yet on the other hand, humour is clearly widely employed as a technique. Something like a quarter of all TV commercials seem to set out to make you laugh. Lots of ads are written with a clear desire to be funny. In British advertising, at least, humour has been a tool in very broad use for many decades.

What does the record suggest? Are there humorous campaigns that have demonstrably worked very well? Are there cases where humour has clearly caused advertising to be unsuccessful?

The answer to those to questions is confusingly, 'Yes' in both cases.

Guinness, for instance, ran delightful ads in which humour played a major part for many, many years. They built the brand. They are still remembered today. They were unquestionably one of the great advertising success stories.

Xerox in the US used humorous TV commercials to put its business products on the map – and were massively successful in doing it. In a few short years the copying business grew and grew, and the Xerox company grew with it to a major company

And the flops? They are too numerous and too fugitive to mention. But think back and I am sure you can remember commercials that made you laugh – and failed totally to impress on you the name of the product being advertised.

In total I suspect there are more unsuccessful, failed humorous campaigns than glittering successes. But then, there are a lot more campaigns of all types that don't work particularly well than there are campaigns that are brilliant exceptions.

Most people will tell you that humour is 'dangerous', 'tricky', 'can backfire'. However, they are not often very specific about how and why.

We need first of all to analyse what humour can actually contribute, before we can decide whether we should employ it or not. And it is, I think, this analysis that is fundamentally lacking

So, what can humour do to make advertising work?

Humour can raise attention and aid memorability

Jokes are remembered. Incongruous or amusing situations stick in your mind and you like to recount them to others. The function of humour in raising attention and increasing memorability is a function we all experience daily.

When humour is employed for this purpose in an advertising there is one key test – *relevance*.

Humorous ads that work use their humour to illustrate and point up the central strategy promise. You cannot remember the joke without remembering the central promise of the ad.

Conversely, if the joke is not relevant, if it is simply added on to a straight commercial, then it actually distracts your attention from the advertising message.

Perhaps this can be well illustrated in two differing commercials for cigars.

The first is Hamlet – one of the great humour success stories. (And incidentally employed in a field, tobacco goods, where humour only has a moderate track record. The 'norm' in tobacco goods of all kinds has always been to project an idealised stereotype and invite the smoker's identification with this person and lifestyle.)

Hamlet does the exact opposite to the norm. It depicts ordinary people in situations of mild embarrassment which, with the simplifications and pointing of art, can be assumed to have had their parallels in the lives of all of us.

The mild frustration and embarrassment experienced then leads the protagonist to seek refuge and relief in smoking a Hamlet cigar.

This scenario does play directly and provably to one of the major reasons for smoking at all. People smoke to 'have something to do with their hands'. Drive into a sudden traffic jam on the motorway and you will see lighters flashing in every car round you. A temporary frustration or embarrassment leads to the release in smoking.

This story, as far as I know, has only been consistently used by one other tobacco goods brand, and that was the German filter cigarette HB which used very similar situations on TV for many years – and was far and away the brand leader for most of that time.

The story is of course not product-specific. It therefore needs a brand in a strong position and with massive resources to pre-empt what is after all a generic function of smoking.

But given that proviso, the Hamlet story (repeated in dozens of delightful little inventive playlets) does dramatise a story relevant to smoking the brand. It has also made the brand very successful.

I would like to contrast this case with another brand of cigars, launched some years ago with an opulent and immaculately filmed commercial. The location was Istanbul. Photography and direction were outstanding. The protagonist was George Cole, playing (impeccably) a rather incompetent secret agent, and the story was as follows. The secret agent in the crowded city street has to pass a document to a contact. He folds the paper into a tiny cylinder and slips it into his pack of cigars (their name I have understandably forgotten). He is approached by a man whom he assumes to be his contact and offers him the cigar packet. The stranger accepts politely. But he takes the cigar and not the little cylinder of paper which is proffered. So Cole forces the cylinder on him. Nonplussed, but not wishing to be impolite, the man takes the cylinder, lights it at a kebab-seller's stall and uses it to light his cigar. Cole is amazed, the wrong man walks off thanking him for the cigar, as the real contact turns up through the crowd.

What makes this story totally different from the Hamlet story is that the product has no significant role to play. The joke is there and it is a good joke and beautifully performed. But the product has no part in it.

So, logically, even though you remember the joke, it cannot help you to remember the product.

Helping the ad to be remembered, is perhaps the major use of humour. Most of the humorous campaigns that do not work fall down on this simple test of relevance.

But there are other functions of humour and it might be as well to look quickly at these, particularly as their role is not anywhere near so well understood.

Humour can make it possible to render the intangible tangible

There is a commercial for Duckham's Oil which features a man on a lonely foggy road, whose car – obviously mistreated by him – stops suddenly. Attempting to get it moving again, he gets out and fetches an anonymous can of oil from the boot. But the car asserts its own will, locks him out and then refuses to let him in. Reason? It wants a proper diet, namely, Duckham's Oil.

British Rail have a commercial where a businessman travelling in a

Figure 24   Hellman's doesn't even need a word to put this joke right on strategy

train experiences all the frustrations that can happen to a motorist – being stopped for speeding, getting into a traffic jam, having to stop to relieve himself – but don't usually happen to passengers in trains.

Both these examples use fantasy to make their point. They show things happening that simply don't happen. But they do it with a certain humour – slightly macabre in the first, more obviously funny in the second. The point of both is to make the intangible tangible. This is a frequent use of humour and a very valid one.

Humour can make a product friendlier and more approachable

Someone once remarked to me that he was quite surprised when he had his first glass of Guinness to find that, unlike the Guinness he had seen in advertisements for years, it did not have a smiling face in the creamy head. One of the most remarkable effects of the classic Guinness advertising was the way in which you came to like the product's personality. You felt it would be good company, good-humoured, always amusing and friendly.

Figure 25 British Rail – a clever use of humour and fantasy

The TV campaign for Legal & General in which the company's spokesman either does (or does not) get drenched works well in reminding you of the visual identity of an umbrella symbol. But perhaps its best advantage is that it makes you see an insurance company – never the most sympathetic or human entity – as friendly and approachable and likeable.

This can be one of the best reasons for using humour but, of course, it demands that the humour you use *is* goodhumoured. You will hardly achieve a more human and sympathetic image if your humour is barbed and sharp. If greater sympathy is your aim, then your humour, like Legal & General's, should be directed against the one person who will not complain – yourself.

Humour can disarm criticism and opposition

The function of advertising is to change the potential customer's mind. How easy or difficult this is to perform depends at least partially on how strongly the present viewpoint is held. Some opinions are very strongly held – like the opinions we have about patriotism, politics, religion, our families and friends. Other opinions – including many of those we have about commercial products – are not held so strongly. Understandably, the opinions we hold strongly are not given up easily. If somebody challenges our deeply-held beliefs our immediate reaction is resentment, indignation, defensiveness and an accusation that the challenger is a liar and probably subversive.

Because decisions about commercial products are usually rather unimportant and superficial, advertising can usually have a stab at changing the potential customer's opinion without having to cope with any strong resentment or anger. But sometimes we *do* need to challenge beliefs. And, if this is the case, then humour can be a powerful ally. It reduces tension, gets both parties to confess their common humanity and makes it easier for the other person to consider your argument rather than simply resorting to an automatic rejection.

A very good example of this is the Health Education Council ad that encourages men to use condoms by asking them, 'Would you be more careful if it was you that got pregnant?' and illustrated by an apparently pregnant man. The picture induces a smile and that, in itself, induces a situation in which one doesn't reject the message out of hand but actually considers it.

You would think – considering its potential for persuading people to take on board and give some attention to a message that they instinctively reject – that this kind of humour would be more used in political advertising. Yet actually it is used very rarely. Humour itself is used and frequently, but it is the savage, annihilating humour of the 'I'm right and you're wrong' school.

The reason for this is a dispiriting but understandable one. Political ads are approved by the converted. They want ads that will sock their opponents where it hurts. That will have their supporters nodding vigorously at their transparent 'rightness'. Unfortunately, these ads are not the ones that cause conversion or attract the floating, uncommitted voter. He is much more likely to be attracted by the kind of humour we have been discussing – the gentle humour that turneth away wrath.

Humour can make emotion 'allowable'

There are occasions when masses of American commercials are shown to large audiences of British creative people. They always expose one great difference in the make-up of the two peoples. There are always a number of commercials in the American reels that are unashamedly emotional.

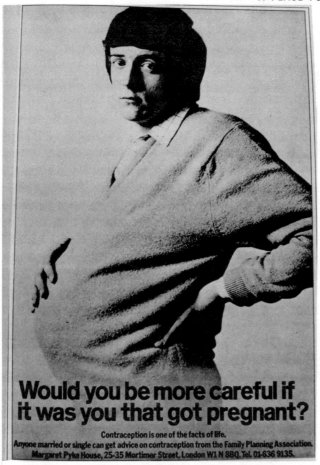

Figure 26 Health Education Council – humour to disarm the reader's resistance

Kodak, particularly, is a master of the art. They glorify family love, nice kids, decent values – and they make British creative people howl with embarrassed laughter.

Now, these commercials would probably not receive such a strong thumbs down if shown to the average British TV audience. But the average audience would, I suspect, be at least a little uncomfortable with them. British diffidence shies away from sentimentality and overt emotion.

Does this mean we should simply discard the powerful emotions as a tool? Hardly, because there are obviously products and communications strategies where they can be of value to us.

155

This is one of the many situations in which humour can help. Humour can take the edge of embarrassment off a situation or appeal that the diffident British find too emotional. Some of the Hovis commercials had this quality.

CHAPTER 26

Techniques of the Art Director

While a lot of people assume that advertisements more or less write themselves, all are clear that an artist has some hand in them. Clearly, the whole thing doesn't just happen on the page.

Just as the copywriter is a member of the team that decides on the fundamentals of the positioning, and the overall nature of the campaign, but also has the specific job of writing the words and the responsibility for this alone, a modern art director is a key member of the team. But he also has a sole responsibility: for putting the ad into its final graphic shape.

There are essentially two parts to this job:

Deciding on the visual elements, the picture or pictures, and arranging for this picture to be shot, drawn, procured or whatever.

Designing the overall ad and campaign and putting its various elements together.

Both these tasks have a major impact on communication, since the illustration is usually as important as the headline in deciding the ad's attention-getting potential, and makes a major contribution to the overall idea it conveys, while the layout has a decisive effect on the general 'feel' that is communicated and the degree of reading which is achieved.

The choice of illustrations

The main illustration, in conjunction with the headline, should ideally communicate the main message of the ad. These two elements will normally be seen by large numbers of readers whereas only a minority (but a very important minority, your predestined customers who are genuinely interested) actually go any further. It follows that the illustration is very important and consequently considerable work has been done in the attempt to classify which types of illustration are of maximum inherent interest.

Given that the greatest interest is self-interest, it is hardly surprising that men look at pictures of men and women look at pictures of women. Babies are very interesting to women but much less so to men. Women's fashions are of interest to women but poison to men. Men's fashions are only of moderate interest to men. Cars are of high interest to men, but only of lower interest to women. Illustrations that show some event, something interesting happening are of high interest to both groups, with men having a high interest in sport and women a higher interest in scenes that have a romantic content. Stars and celebrities are of high interest to both.

Quite apart from the subject matter of illustrations there are some formal considerations which are very significant. Photographs attract much more attention than drawings, so much so that a drawing of an interesting subject will probably score below a photograph of a less interesting one. If drawings or illustrations are used, they will usually score higher the more realistic or photographic they are. Abstract art is death to any widespread interest.

Photographs attract their highest attention when they are comparatively large (more than half the area of the ad), printed with background and straight sides, not cut out to make an unusual shape. They are usually most effective if there is sufficient background visible to make orientation easy and suggest a kind of reality – the extreme close-up is rarely very effective.

Once again we should not simply take these statements to heart without questioning them. Only by understanding why these reactions occur and recur can we be reasonably sure that we are illustrating the right things in the right way.

The preference for photographs and for photographs in a typically reportage format reflects the simple fact that this is the way in which we receive most of our information. Newspapers use photographs more or less exclusively. The TV screen is a squared-up photograph.

The preference for certain subjects is also understandable if you appreciate that we do not look at pictures, we look at subjects. A photographer will photograph a baby and be pleased at the way the light falls on the hair. A printer will be pleased at his success in holding subtle half-tones in the flesh. A reader will look at it and say, 'My sister's little boy looks like that.' The reason why abstract art, or even art which is very strongly stylised, generally does not produce much interest in advertisements is that the technique gets in the way of the subject. Abstract art forces you to think about art, when you want to know what the picture depicts.

It is obviously easiest to project ourselves into a picture if it is sufficiently clear and has sufficient verisimilitude for us to build up an idea of the world it depicts. It is easiest to put ourselves into that picture if the protagonist is someone with whom we can identify and if that protagonist is doing something which we find interesting, attractive, enjoyable or exciting.

It is always good if you can achieve a picture which has some 'story' content, which arouses the wish to know why exactly what is shown is happening. This is often some quite small factor. The famous eyepatch worn by the Hathaway shirt model somehow suggested that something interesting had happened somewhere – it made Hathaway a major brand in an unprecedentedly short time and on a remarkably low budget.

You will find that editors apply the same criteria to the pictures (virtually exclusively photographs, as we have noted) that they put in their papers and magazines. They know the rules that govern interest and attention.

> If the client sobs and sighs,
> Make the name-block twice the size.
> If he still should prove refractory,
> Put in a picture of the factory.
> Only in the gravest case
> Illustrate the client's face.

This piece of doggerel has been around agencies since the 1930s at least. It is a reminder of the inherent difference in emphasis between the advertiser and the art director. It recognises that the advertiser has an abiding concern that the advertisement he is paying for will in fact help his business. He is concerned that the advertisement be clearly branded (hence the oversized name-block). He takes it for granted that the product being sold will be a dominant presence in the advertisement. He is likely to think that the factory which is his pride and joy is capable of arousing the same intense admiration among his customers. (The final couplet recognises that, when the crisis of confidence has reached a point where the loss of the account is imminent, it is hard for anyone to turn down an advertisement in which their own features play a leading role.)

159

The art director, inevitably, has somewhat different concerns and emphases. He is likely to want to keep the ad simple and graphically chaste – sometimes at the expense of branding. He is likely to want to show pictures that are attractive – perhaps sometimes at the expense of relevance. He is creating something which in a very real sense is *his*, even though somebody else may be paying for it.

This is a long-standing confrontation and it is unlikely to go away. It is also clear that both sides have a legitimate case. In a cluttered media world, ads do need to be strongly branded. It is not unreasonable that the product that is offered for sale should be shown. On the other hand, ads will only communicate if they enter the 'you' world of the reader and do not remain in the 'we' world of the manufacturer.

So how does one work out the rights and wrongs of the confrontation in particular cases? Can the apparently contradictory points made by both parties be subsumed into a logical scheme?

One hesitates to point again to the copy strategy as a sovereign panacea, but defining the promise to be made will also automatically steer the art director towards a sensible illustration, and perhaps also work against the client demanding an inappropriate one.

Product illustrations are legitimate and are in fact very commonly used where one of two factors apply.

- Where the product's appearance is a major argument in its purchase and hence its appearance is vitally required information.
- Where the product has a special visible feature which is key to its performance.

From this it will be clear why pictures of the product are virtually universal in fashion ads and in car ads. They are also often used for technical products or where the aim is to explain a technical feature. However the style of the illustration is different in this case. It aims at clarity and often concentrates on details. In the first case, the illustration concentrates on making the product look as desirable as possible. It also often surrounds the product with other signs of a particular lifestyle.

Illustrations that show the result of using the product are understandably used for functional products like household appliances, cleaning products and food products but also for cosmetics and toiletries and wherever the product itself is not the object of desire but the job it performs.

Obviously such illustrations can vary from the close-up shot of a dish prepared with somebody's flour to a large-scale shot of a house decorated with a certain brand of paint. Equally obviously the lifestyle connotations of the picture can be very minor or they can be almost overwhelming.

Illustrations showing the ideal consumer are often utilised for products of conspicuous consumption (they were very common for cigarettes before the restrictions made it more or less impossible to show any people in the ads) for the sufficient reason that emulation of a particular type of person is an important reason in the choice of such products. They are also often used for impulse products, mainly as a device for flagging a particular type of audience rather than with the aim of emulation or identification.

Illustrating the client's face is not, as the doggerel would suggest, a last resort of flattery. It can be a valid executional device if

- The company has an image that is otherwise impersonal and unfriendly.
- The founder or whoever is depicted can be made to represent a key quality in the product – like fussy, old-fashioned Mr Brain whose faggots are made with great care.
- The founder really does come over well. If he is a natural – like

Figure 27 Bernard Matthews – illustrating the client's face successfully

Bernard Matthews or Victor Kiam – he is a lot more believable than any hired spokesman.

Branding

An ad is said to be strongly branded if it communicates the name of the product behind the ad strongly. Obviously, branding is desirable in virtually any ad, but there are categories where it is more important than in others.

- Impulse products require strong branding because of the nature of the purchase – it is unconsidered and the product is bought simply because the brand is in the forefront of the mind.
- Routine purchases also benefit from strong branding for the same reason.
- Challenging brands need to be strongly branded if they face a very dominant market leader. This is simply due to the tendency for readers to ascribe all advertising in a particular category to the market leader.

Given that there is a need for strong branding, the art director and the client are then typically likely to fall out over how to achieve it. The client's technique will be: 'Make the name-block twice the size'. The art director may go about it more subtly but ultimately more effectively. Strongly branded campaigns often use distinctive style elements and visual techniques to good effect. The danger, of course, is that they become so unconventional and stylised that they cannot communicate the breadth of material that a campaign has to cover.

The techniques of good layout

The art director's other job is designing the ad so that it communicates. Here a great mass of detailed knowledge has been gathered over the years.

Overall, ads are best noticed and read if they marshal the information they offer in a way that makes it easy for the reader to assimilate it. Essentially, this means using the visual grammar that editors use and to which we have all become accustomed.

Illustrations, as we have noted, should be squared up and ideally constitute somewhat over 50 per cent of the ad. A dominant headline should be placed underneath the picture (reading is less if it is above the picture). The headline should be set in upper and lower case, particularly if it is more than a few words in length. Under no circumstances should body copy be reversed out of a picture since it greatly hampers reading. Headlines reversed out of a picture also suffer but, if they are short, only to a comparatively negligible degree. Copy should be set neatly, in a size at least as large as the publication in which the ad appears normally uses. Drop capitals (the large initial letters at the beginning of a chapter) aid readership. The measure (the length of each individual line) should not be greater than the publication typically employs.

Subheads increase reading as do all devices for adding emphasis in lengthy copy. Pictures should be captioned since the reading of captions is high and the attention paid to the picture greater.

There are also some factors peculiar to advertising that the art director needs to have mastered, such as:

Pictorial comparisons. Be they 'before and after' or 'our product versus their product', it is essential that they be placed side by side to enable horizontal reading. Placed one above the other they will not usually be seen as a comparison at all. It is also wise to stress the comparability by keeping the pictures to the same size and as much as possible to the same angle – in other words the pictures should be as congruent as possible since this throws up the incongruity of the difference you are selling. The comparison seems to work better if the undesirable result is on the left and the desirable one on the right – we progress from bad to good, from 'Before' to 'After'.

Coupons. Because coupons are often put into ads as a comparative afterthought (perhaps insisted on by the client while also demanding that the name block be larger), they often get placed in the bottom right-hand corner. They will however attract the highest redemption if they are in the most conspicuous place possible – and that usually means centred in the top half of the advertisement. If coupon redemption is the main purpose of the ad, then it is always right to make the coupon central to the ad and draw attention to it in the headline.

Pack-shots. These are obligatory if the product itself is not the main illustration. They should be three-dimensionally shot, not depicted as flat designs, and it is often better to put them into their own squared-up picture rather than to isolate them on the white page.

Figure 28 If there's a coupon in your ad, put it in the centre

> Logos are usually better understood if they appear as part of some three-dimensional object – for instance, showing a pump head or a banner with the Esso sign on it, rather than just the flat design itself.

The final thing that art directors need to realise is that they are working for the finished ad in the newspaper or magazine. The layout pinned on the conference room wall and attracting the enthusiastic support of the entire meeting is not what it's all about. This, unfortunately, can often get forgotten.

One symptom is the tendency of creative people to opt for giant spaces – full pages in newspapers, double-page spreads in magazines. These giant spaces are not without problems since they tend to be banned to the less desirable positions in the newspaper or magazine, thus making a nonsense of using a particular medium because of its prized reader involvement and editorial content. The use of giant spaces also wastes money. A space unit that occupies two-thirds or three-quarters of a newspaper page is just as well-noticed as, and significantly cheaper than, a full page. One-and-a-half page units do just as well in magazines as double page spreads when it comes to attention, but again they are significantly cheaper.

Another symptom of thinking no further than the approved layout is artwork that is hard to reproduce adequately because its photographic subtlety is too much for the reproduction techniques of the medium being used. A similar fault leads to ads that must have looked great as flat layouts but look a lot less than great in a book that is bound so that it cannot be opened out completely. When half the car or most of the action disappears into the gutter, then it must be questioned if the client is getting value for money.

CHAPTER 27

The Techniques of TV

TV (and radio and cinema, for that matter) are totally different from print in their creative demands. This is because the advertisement in these media exists in time and not in space.

You buy these media in units of time – 20, 30 and (if you're feeling very expansive) 40 or even 60 second units. This fact makes for some important differences.

1. The number of words you can say are strictly limited. Even if you use every available second and a fast-talking announcer, 30 seconds can only hold some 70 words – 50 would be a more normal average.

2. All these comparatively few words get broadly similar emphasis. While 'supering' (using titles printed on the screen) can certainly add emphasis, there is no distinction comparable to the great difference between headline and body copy in the typical press ad.

3. This means that there is no way to accommodate the subsidiary, minor arguments, the supporting sales points that can be tucked away in print ads.

4. The advertisement is presented to all viewers – there is no way to flag the interested parties and let the others turn the page. Once the ad is running it runs its allotted seconds before every member of the audience.

5. Whereas in a press ad you have to attract the people to read, in TV they are already watching (more or less) and what you have to do is stop them turning their attention off. It is a difference of degree only, but it makes for different techniques.

6. The advertisement dictates its own speed of assimilation. Those

members of the audience who are quick on the uptake cannot speed it up, those who are slow or who would like to go back over a particular point, have no way to do so.

Dramatising your copy strategy

Writing good TV commercials comes down to finding a dramatic translation of the copy strategy. People who know nothing about the medium assume that an award-winning director or a brilliant lighting cameraman will give them a powerful commercial. This is nonsense. These highly-paid wizards are essentially film technicians and they are helpless if they do not have a good script to work their wizardry on. A good script, on the other hand, given merely run-of-the-mill competence in its realisation, will always work.

The best TV commercials are like good jokes. They have a story. They can be recounted to people who have not seen them, just as good jokes can, and they still make sense and engage interest. They are economical, well-formed, single-minded communicative bullets and their virtue lies in their penetration.

To show you what I mean let me quote some (admittedly not genuine) comments that viewers might have said about commercials that are often visible on our screens.

'An Englishman was engaged to a French girl and when he was introduced to her father it was a disaster, but he gave him Piat d'Or wine and it all worked out.'

'A man was in a car wash showing how the Knirps umbrella could stand up to rough treatment.'

'There was a businessman travelling on a train and the train got in a jam and he was pulled over for speeding – all the things that can happen in a car.'

'Alan Whicker in the Wild West. People were getting thrown out of the saloons but he could get what he wanted with his Barclaycard.'

'There was this bear in the pub dressed up like a man and showing off how good he was at pub games. He drinks Hofmeister.'

'They showed a double-barrelled shotgun being loaded and fired. It's a new pain-killer and it has two ingredients instead of just one.'

'It was a film out of the 1920s or 1930s in a pub and it said how Courage beer still tasted like that.'

'There was a woman whose dog had won at Crufts and she said she always fed him Pedigree Chum.'

These are very simple little stories – single sentences with 20 to 30 words – yet I expect you recognise the commercials described. You will also notice that, if a thought as simple as this has been lodged in your mind, you have actually absorbed the copy strategy. And the reason why you have absorbed the strategy is that it has not merely been stated, it has, in fact been dramatised for you. It has become the centre of a short memorable story. If you remember the story you must remember the product's strategy because it is inextricably interwoven with the story – you cannot remember one and forget the other.

In fact, the commercials I have mentioned above are all of different types. The Piat d'Or commercial is a representative of a category described in the industry as slice-of-life. The Knirps commercial (a beautiful little piece of salesmanship, it's only a pity they don't have the money to show it more often!) is a straight presenter demonstration commercial. The British Rail commercial is an excellent example of film fantasy, whereas Alan Whicker in the Wild West is an example of the celebrity commercial. Hofmeister's bear is an example of a continuing character identified with the product. Solpadeine is a filmic metaphor. Courage is really just a musical commercial. Pedigree Chum is a straight testimonial. We can use these commercials to learn a little about how the various types of commercial are constructed and how they work.

Slice-of-life

Commercials using this format are little playlets in which characters enact a story in which the advertised product has an important role. The constraints of time (about 50 words in a 30 second commercial, remember, and 30 seconds is now the norm) and the need to do justice to the product, tend to impose some fairly draconian restrictions on this type of commercial.

The characters need to be readily understood people in a readily understood situation. This is simply because the time and words required to

explain an unfamiliar situation, develop more rounded characteri-
sation and so on are simply not available. Even so, in the days when
this type of commercial was developed and when commercials were
typically 60 seconds in length, the extremely simple situation and cast
usually proved best. It demands less of the viewer if the basic situation
and the people are essentially familiar and can be established in a
phrase – 'A nervous young Englishman being introduced to his
prospective French father-in-law', 'A schoolteacher and the cheeky
boy in the class', 'The young wife and the domineering mother in
law'. It is no accident that the openings of good slice-of-life
commercials are like the opening lines of jokes – just as in jokes, we
need to know instantly where we are and what to expect.

There needs to be some kind of conflict between the protagonists. All drama
starts from some kind of conflict which then reaches a resolution.
Naturally, the conflict can be more serious and drawn-out in *King Lear*
than it can in a 30 second commercial, but at least a mild
disagreement, or the opposition of one person who knows about the
product and one who does not is vital in the structure of such a
commercial. If both characters (and this type of commercial needs a
minimum of two, though it can rarely afford the time for more than
three) are completely agreed about the product and simply vie with
each other in praising it, you have a commercial that no-one wants to
watch, that almost certainly only *relates* rather than *dramatises* the copy
strategy and which will not function dramatically.

A recent Pirelli commercial was set in a glamorous, upmarket world
reminiscent of *Dynasty* and had a wife tampering with her husband's
car brakes so that when he set off only the superb road-holding of his
Pirelli tyres thwarted the Grim Reaper. This is the only commercial I
have ever met that utilises a conflict as serious as attempted murder,
so I cannot be sure what sort of reactions viewers might have. I
suspect that it might be found to have shattered the convention and be
rejected for this reason.

Most of the situations in which slice-of-life is played out are clearly
derived from the more humble soap operas like *Coronation Street* or from
situation comedies, and the use of stock characters in stock situations
stresses this ancestry and favours minor day-to-day problems. The
fact that the products advertised in this way are often humble
household items like detergents, cleaners or food products also tends
to favour a simple domestic environment and concentration on
problems and disagreements that such products can conceivably

influence. When totally different type of product use this format then, understandably, the setting will be different – a good example is the Hanson Trust commercials that show a typically slice-of-life confrontation between an American and an Englishman in a business atmosphere.

The product must have a central, problem solving role in the commercial. This is implicit in the injunction to dramatise the copy strategy and is the most important distinction between successful and unsuccessful commercials of this type. It is also the reason why some element of conflict is needed not just on legitimate dramatic grounds but on advertising grounds as well. The product must not merely be present, it must actively bring about the solution. The Piat d'Or wine does this in our example. The schoolteacher's Sinex enables him to give the naughty boy his come-uppance. The Pirelli driver's tyres enable him to outwit his would-be Clytemnestra. One does, however, see a number of commercials which are witty, well-acted, beautifully directed – and where the product has no central role at all.

Continuing character commercials

For understandable reasons, continuing characters generally appear in slice-of-life commercials. Their role is to add recognition and distinctiveness. Since it is now getting harder and harder for advertisers to afford strong, month-in, month-out campaigns the role of the continuing character is becoming reduced. An obvious way to make greater use of the technique – which has an excellent track record – is to add radio commercials for frequency to the television commercials which would establish the character.

A continuing character usually plays the 'expert' role in a slice-of-life commercial, showing novices how to solve their problems by using the product. It follows that the character needs to have some sort of expertise. It is equally vital that the character should be a *character* – ie a strongly-defined memorable person with a typical way of speaking, typical clothing and appearance, strongly held opinions and antipathies.

Demonstration commercials

These have an honourable pedigree and have been around since the earliest days of television. In fact, they have been around since pitchmen sold kitchen implements with a fast spiel and a rapid demonstration from barrows outside Gamages.

Because such commercials tend to concentrate on how the product works and on proving that it actually does work they are usually used for products of a functional nature and with a strong product positioning. Because they tend to dramatise the second paragraph of the copy strategy rather than the first, such commercials have often been incorporated in other commercials where they form a common demonstration sequence while opening and close are varied. This is a practice that gets quite difficult within the constraints of 30 seconds even though it could usually be managed in a minute. The result is that today, regrettably, demonstrations seem to be on the decline. I can only assume that they will come back again, since they are powerful selling tools that use the innate strengths of television superbly. A few pointers about demonstration commercials:

a. *Tie word and picture closely together.* You need to tell people what they are seeing as they see it otherwise they may miss the point. The actual demonstration should be shot in close up so that viewers can see exactly what is going on.

b. *Choose the right kind of demonstration.* There are many. In a *Simple demonstration*, we just take a good look at the product doing its work through the eyes of an unobtrusive camera. The emphasis is on believability – the camera cannot lie.

In a *comparative demonstration*, we see our product and a competitor doing their work side-by-side or one after the other if we need the full screen. Perhaps we go on seeing the competitor working long after we have finished – in which case our half of the screen may be used for a totally different picture such as the relaxation after the job is complete.

A *larger-than-life demonstration* uses the miracle of film to show us things that the eye normally cannot see – by magnifying the process, by seeing inside something normally sealed up, by using slow motion or by speeding the process up.

The 'torture test' is a demonstration that says, in effect, 'this product can do anything you would want it to do, because it can do this which is way beyond the normal call of duty.' Examples are: piling six Volvos on top of each other to show that the body is strong, Tonka toys having an elephant stand on top of a toy tractor, Remington's shaving a peach and then a bristle brush to make the two points 'gentle to skin' and 'tough on your beard'.

c. *Experiment with your demonstration*. Effective demonstration is not easy. Do not assume that you are going to get it right first time. It is well worth while undertaking some experimental work with a video camera before you do the final version, finding out which are the most effective angles and the most effective way to play it. Props, for instance, can make an enormous difference. Band-Aid wished to show how its sticking plaster stuck instantly and found a demonstration lifting an egg out of boiling water. If they had chosen something else, something less smooth and less at home in boiling water, the demonstration would have been less effective.

d. *Brand your demonstration*. One of the problems of a demonstration commercial used, as they often are, to introduce a radical new product, is that as imitators of the product come along (as they surely will), they will also imitate your commercial. This can be resisted – and general retention and understanding and identification can be increased if the commercial is consciously branded. Do your demonstration with props that are unique to you, in a way or in a location that is unique to you, with your brand name and logo clearly visible and hopefully playing some key role.

Shell showed that a car filled with its petrol went further than a car in which the special Shell ingredient was not present. It could have just showed one car stopped and the other still running. In fact, the point where the first car stopped was marked by a marker through which the Shell car burst. A generic demonstration had become a Shell-specific one.

Fantasy and metaphor

I have separated these two before but they are closely related. The technique, in both cases, is to use filmic methods to make something which is abstract, or hard to show or hard to explain, more concrete and real to the viewer. For instance, to explain how the enzyme-inhibitor in a toothpaste works, an announcer explains while behind him a boy threatens to spray him with a hose. The water is turned on and – lo and behold – he is in fact separated from the mischievous *arroseur* by a plate of glass. This I class as a metaphor. Fantasy, on the other hand, is the metaphor that takes over the commercial and places it in its special world. The driver who finds trains behaving the same way as motor traffic does is a good example.

These types of commercial are generally, because of their deliberate unreality, distinctive and arresting. They are very properly used where the copy strategy point to be dramatised is simply not concrete. The rapid growth in financial advertising and service advertising, where the product is essentially intangible, is likely to increase the popularity of this type of commercial.

They have two potential problems that should be considered:

a. *The metaphor must be understandable.* If it is too far-fetched, too hard to comprehend then people will simply not realise what is happening.

b. *The solution and not the problem must be the subject of the metaphor.* This is a problem frequently ignored. The protagonist says 'I feel like I'm a thousand years old' and, thanks to the make-up department, instantly appears a thousand years old. All this (I hope fictitious) commercial has done is dramatise the problem. It can easily be ascribed to any other competitive product and probably will be.

Musical commercials

These have also been around since things began. The key thing to remember with them is that the use of music does not release one from the obligations of selling. In a good musical commercial, music is generally no more than an added plus of memorability to what would be a good commercial anyway. It adds atmosphere and, by connecting words to a memorable melody, anchors the words in your mind.

Bad musical commercials are simply bad commercials – where creative people have simply given way to the temptation to play Oscar Hammerstein and Busby Berkeley with the client's money.

Celebrity commercials

Much of what we have said about musical commercials applies to this category too. The use of a celebrity is justified when:

a. *The celebrity is a known authority on the subject.* This is the situation with racing drivers talking about petrol and tyres, tennis stars endorsing tennis equipment and so on.

b. *The celebrity adds image and conviction values.* Certain people add a personal dimension to a product they endorse. They are known reporters on the subject or related subjects – René Cutforth on

Figure 29   A believable testimonial from Orson Welles

Australia, Alan Whicker on the role of the Barclaycard in the USA –
so they have a reporter's authority and apparent truthfulness and
conviction. Alternatively they sum up in themselves the sort of image
you want to identify with your product. A good example of the latter
were the commercials Orson Welles made for Domecq and those that
various celebrities have made for the *Guardian*.

Apart from these situations, the use of a celebrity to attract
attention and to give polish, form and function to a thoroughly bad
commercial is exactly comparable to the use of music to do a similar
job.

A parallel point has to be made. If you buy an expensive person, do
not assume the creative problem has been solved. A celebrity
commercial still needs to have an idea and a structure that dramatises
the copy strategy and thus communicates it. The celebrity can be very
effective but only if integrated into the real purpose of the commercial.

Candid testimonials

There is also a long tradition of real people in commercials. Detergents particularly have used them frequently over the years and they are favoured by all products that have believability as a major aim. Often they are simply used to say that they like the product – this, of course, is not a dramatisation of the copy strategy. Using real people effectively seems to be dependent on two factors:

a. *Establishing real authenticity.* This is often a question of time: of devoting enough time and footage to the testimonial person for them to come across as real and believable. In shooting commercials with real people it is normal to overshoot considerably and assemble the commercial from a comparative wealth of material, an interview of 10 or 15 minutes' duration being required for 10 seconds of finished film. Interviewers are usually necessary since most non-professionals cannot act spontaneously and talk easily to the camera, they need questions to react to. That said, the art of cutting these commercials is to get as much of the testimonial and as little as the interviewer as possible.

b. *Imposing a structure on the commercials.* Interviews with the general public are often very rambling if they remain interviews. Effective campaigns ask people to do things and thus impose a structure on the amorphous interview. The detergent field is full of excellent examples – asking a woman to pick the pile of laundry that is whiter, asking her to try an anonymous packet of detergent not knowing what brand it is, asking her if she would swap the new powder you have introduced her to for two packets of the one she used to swear by.

Simple dramatic tricks of this kind ensure that the testimonials achieved are in line with the product's copy strategy. They also ensure that there is a genuine dramatic structure to the commercial rather than just a cosy chat – that there is the tension of an initial disagreement and the resolution provided by the product.

All TV commercials have some things in common, and it is probably best to finish this discussion of an effective and intrusive medium by stressing a few things which are common to all commercials that use it.

- Direct speech – where somebody photographed by the camera and visible to you speaks directly to you – is usually much better registered than voice-over.
- Because commercials are so short it is desirable to establish the name of the product early on. Sometimes, witholding the name

of the product can be a deliberate dramatic device as in the 'mystery pack' detergent campaign we have just mentioned. It is only justifiable if the product is very well known.

● Most viewers give most of their attention to the picture on TV; the words are subordinate. Try to be sure that the pictures tell the story you wish to tell.

● For the same reason be sure that the words you say relate closely to what the video is showing. If there is a discrepancy it will always be the pictures that win out.

CHAPTER 28

Techniques of Cinema and Radio

These two media share the important characteristic of existing in time and not in space with TV. However, as media, they are very different and this leads to some (I believe essentially minor) differences in their employment.

TV has been a mainstream medium, taking a major percentage of major advertisers' spend more or less since its establishment. It gives virtually complete coverage of most people in Britain on a regional basis and with an acceptable frequency. Radio and cinema are very different. Radio as an advertising medium is essentially local and still fairly new in most areas. It is heavily used by local advertisers whereas national advertisers tend to regard it as a support medium only. Cinema is heavily skewed towards the younger age groups with large numbers of older people virtually never visiting the cinema. Again it is a support medium rather than a mainstream medium.

These media have considerably greater significance in some other countries. Radio is a powerful medium in those countries where the tradition of commercial broadcasting is well established such as the US and Australia, or where TV is either lacking or artificially limited – West Germany is such a case. Cinema is still a powerful medium in many Middle East countries.

In creative terms, the primary rule of TV applies without reservation to cinema and radio, namely dramatise the copy strategy. Thereafter some minor differences are evident.

Cinema *could* use exactly the same commercials shot for TV, but most advertisers seem to feel that a special film is necessary. This stems from the fact that people visit the cinema for entertainment, and specifically the entertainment provided by feature films, whereas television provides a complete gamut of entertainment, current affairs, news, practical interests like cookery and gardening and so on. The audience has paid a significant sum to come in and the huge screen and the presence of a large audience makes it really impossible for them to ignore a commercial the way they can ignore one at home. This all combines to encourage advertisers who use the medium on a large scale to shoot special films which generally aim for considerable entertainment value. The story content is often high, the commercials are long – typically much longer than the 30-second TV norm – and they use such expensive and expansive devices as major stars, Cinemascope, costly location shoots and so on.

This reaction has never been proved to be right. Generally the audience reached by cinema is also reached by TV and it makes elementary sense to have a strong continuity of theme in the two media and to use a medium which is technically very similar to tell the same story in the same way.

A case could certainly be made for some reshooting or variant shooting. The relationship of the viewer to the screen is very different in TV and cinema and TV usually shoots everything much closer. The extreme close-ups that are often very effective in TV are simply overwhelming and in some cases ununderstandable on the big screen, while we have all seen traditional movies on TV where long shots that worked in the cinema are barely decipherable.

Because cinema has a large audience all sitting in the same place, a vocally critical reaction can much more easily occur. We have all seen commercials familiar from TV, where they seem to be accepted without difficulty, get an embarrassed belly-laugh in the cinema.

Radio is a special case in Britain simply because of the long entrenched position of the BBC in sound broadcasting. The medium is undoubtedly powerful and effective, but the British stations suffer from the omnipresent, highly professional and very varied competition offered by the BBC. The BBC has programmes that are designed for the youthful, pop-music segment, the middle-of-the-road music-with-a-bit-of-talk-segment appealing to a broad C2D audience, the middle-class talk-and-news segment, the highbrow classical music segment and, in addition, a regional network that more or less matches the regional commercial stations. It is hardly suprising if, faced with such competition, the local stations find it hard to get the audience they need to live.

In markets where radio is a major medium, it has often been built by stations segmenting the market on the basis of audience taste. Obviously this is most likely to function in major metropolitan markets, but such markets can then offer news-only stations, music-only stations and other such segmentations. In Britain, the local stations are more or less forced to define themselves as all-purpose, mass media competing essentially with the local paper and going for a broad cross-section of the available audience. This, in its turn, cuts them off from one of the great strengths of radio which is that its very low programming costs can make audience segmentation a feasible and rewarding strategy.

The radio stations have also made a fundamental error in stressing their cheapness as media. This has led to a situation where the great mass of commercials that run on local radio are also produced and written by the local station. The production is barely competent while the writing consistently fails to take any advantage of the tremendous possibilities inherent in a medium where the performance takes place in the listener's mind.

Radio is like TV in its breadth of programming. Like TV it covers everything, it does not limit itself to the fictional story as cinema tends to do. It is a medium with a strong news bent, an affinity for music, an excellent documentary capability, the ability to handle all sorts of drama, and a strong tradition of humour. How few radio commercials take any advantage of these different strands of radio!

Yet, of course, the chance to produce the inventive, unusual radio commercial is far more readily forthcoming than it would be for a TV commercial. Film production is annihilatingly expensive and this fact often leads to good ideas being discarded and to a decision to go on using the commercial that already exists.

Even the most lavish radio commercial, on the other hand, can be rapidly and inexpensively produced. The Charge of the Light Brigade is only two half coconuts, the spaceship crashing on the moon is a couple of voices and some electronic sounds, and the big scene at Waterloo station at the time of the Boer War is some sound effects on record. All you need for a good radio commercial is a good script. This, unfortunately, is what is mostly lacking.

My first recommendation to the would-be radio writer would be to buy himself some records of *The Goon Show*. These will show you what I believe is the hardest thing to master in radio – producing a lively, varied, interest-arousing *texture*. The fundamental rules of dramatising the copy strategy are just the same as in TV – with the added plus for the writer that it is all in words and sound so the dominance of the picture does not take place.

Talking of TV, we mentioned that increasing costs were having a number of effects – restricting the number of commercials made, tending to limit the proven benefit of the continuing character in that medium. Now intelligent use of radio can help solve some of those problems. It can add frequency and variety to your TV campaign. It has been shown that the same basic commercial, used in both media, communicates the pictures of the TV film to the listener who is hearing it on radio. A strong relation between these two media is both possible and desirable.

It may well be that the establishment of further national radio networks will finally make radio the medium it has never really become in Britain, but clearly has the potential to be: a major medium with tremendous creative possibilities.

CHAPTER 29

Techniques of Posters and Direct Mail

These are two media with absolutely opposed characteristics. One is the absolute acme of compression and economy of word and picture, the other positively seeks fullness of selling argument and carries a lot of carefully-judged, personally addressed copy.

The two media are also used for very different products. Posters are common for impulse products and other well-known brands that are in wide distribution, are bought by a broad cross-section of the public and whose sale depends more on establishing awareness and a simple message rather than a detailed, comprehensive sales argument.

Direct mail, on the other hand, is often used by companies who have no other advertising apart from this very private medium. It does little for broad awareness, so is used for products for which that dimension is comparatively unimportant. What it does do superbly is address personally a selected person who may be considered a predestined target for the product in question. It is therefore particularly used by products that are sold direct to the public, and more and more advertisers are now using it to add extra weight in their campaigns for specific target consumers.

In terms of their creative exploitation, the two media are also very different. Posters seek the quick, memorable, slogan-based, primarily visual sale. Direct mail is a medium where the copywriter is king – words carry the burden of information and selling.

Eight rules for good posters

1. Encapsulate the copy strategy.

If you cannot communicate the heart of the copy strategy in one picture and about six words, then the poster medium is not right for your product. (An exception is to be made for those posters opposite the platforms on the London Underground, and the tube cards in the trains themselves – they get longer attention simply because the travellers are captive and there are no windows to look out of. They can really be treated like magazine ads.)

2. Identify the brand clearly.

Since what the poster can communicate is so limited, it is important that – at the very least – the brand is communicated.

3. Put the key words where they can be seen.

Sounds obvious? The lower third of many posters are often obscured by parked cars. Get the key message in the top half.

4. Clear, bright primary colours on white work best.

Perhaps it is our often overcast skies, perhaps it is the fact that posters often have to do their work after dark – the evidence is clear that a white background is very desirable and that colours should be unsubtle.

5. Avoid abstract artwork.

Just as abstract artwork is death to ads, it rarely seems to work in posters too. This despite the Continental school of people like Savignac whose clever posters are the admiration of designers. Photography is best in posters and realistic, readily understood artwork is next best.

6. Be provocative.

Posters must be *quick*. Whereas ads can take their time to identify the audience and involve them, posters need to shock you into attention. As an attention-getter in an ad 'Down with Guinness! Then you'll feel better' would have been inexcusable, in the poster world it works.

7. Aim for a consistent 'look'.

With the urgent need to encapsulate and the need to be provocative, to ask for consistency as well may seem to be gilding the lily. Perrier's posters with their repeated plays on the word 'eau' are proof that it can be done.

8. Tie your poster into the overall campaign.

Posters communicate to more people at lower cost than any other medium. They are ideal for getting a lot of breadth and repetition into your campaign even if the main selling job is being done by TV commercials or press ads. Obviously if this strategy is to work the two have to be associated in the consumer's mind. This means making the poster a summary of the verbal and visual content of the whole campaign.

Moving to the very different medium of direct mail, it is important to say here that the collection of experience and response-building wrinkles built up by the direct marketing specialists would fill and have filled a number of books. Because the response to the medium can be so precisely measured, there is an almost limitless list of factors that affect response and we can only pick on some fundamentals here.

The most fundamental point of all is *the need for good writing that is able to engage the prospect's attention, interests and sympathy and provoke him into action.* This is a medium that attracts punctilious, careful writers with a skill with words, it is not a job for the superficial slogan-writer. That said, let us look at some other factors that affect this medium.

Eight Rules for successful direct mail

1. Get the right address list and test it.

Unlike a broad advertising campaign in traditional media where you may be surprised by response from people you had not reckoned on, it stands to reason that the best direct mail campaign can only be as effective as the list it is sent to. Effective direct mail shots are usually costly in comparison with other media even if they are all properly targeted. The provenance of a list should be carefully investigated (for instance if it purports to give you the names of people in a profession like estate agency and yet is not, when checked out, as up-to-date as the Yellow Pages, then it is clearly not worth much). It should then be tested: a small percentage of the addresses at random mailed and investigated and the return noted. It is unlikely that the test return will be bettered in a complete mailing.

2. Use every technique possible to personalise your mail.

Nowadays the computer and the laser printer have made perfect personalisation possible. (They have not made the business any cheaper!) The rapid growth of direct mail has also meant that nowadays the typical 'circular' of old sticks out like a sore thumb and gets consigned to the wastepaper basket unopened. If you want your mailer to look like a personal letter then it needs to be very carefully designed and every detail weighed. If you are not worried that it be identified as a commercial mailing, then it still needs to look personal and interesting.

3. Successful direct mail copy is long and repetitive.

We have all noticed this fact. Perhaps we should ask ourselves why repetition and wordiness seems to help communication here whereas we generally seek to avoid it. The reason, I suspect, is that many mailers are skimmed over, read in bursts, laid aside, reread and considered before they are finally responded to. Even filling in your name and address and putting the Freepost envelope in the letter box is, after all, a fairly lengthy decision making process. During this comparatively long period, the initial mailer is probably looked at many times and it benefits if, each time, a new argument pops out or a new way of looking at the matter emerges. This can only be a theory – but the fact remains that effective mailers consist of three or four items, each of which repeat the main argument and add their own contribution.

4. Attempt to involve your recipient in the mailing.

If involvement is of value in ordinary ads, it is particularly effective in the concentrated one-to-one atmosphere of a mailer. Involvement can be achieved by the ubiquitous scratch-off fields that show you whether you have won something or not. In a more sophisticated way, it can be achieved, for instance,

- by enclosing sealed envelopes that answer specific questions the recipient may have,
- by asking him to complete survey information or asking for his opinion,
- by offering him a prize for returning a form,
- by offering him some special status. (If he has bought something from you before then he will realise this is the source of his name and address. There is no harm in capitalising on this since previous customers are almost always better prospects than total strangers.)

5. Use the envelope.

Most direct mail comes in an envelope, and a lot comes in envelopes that are unimaginative to say the least. Effective use of the envelope as a way to get the shot opened and to the right person is often neglected. One nice thought – a note to the businessman's secretary on the envelope in shorthand. In the same section we might well consider the extra attraction of an envelope that comes from abroad with a foreign stamp.

6. Encourage rapid response.

A mailshot loses its immediacy just like any other advertisement. For this reason it is necessary to get people to respond quickly, if they are to respond at all. Stimuli for quick response can include such things as a prize if you post before a certain date, attractive conditions that soon lapse or that are only open to the first so-many respondents.

7. Avoid duplication or conflicting messages.

Receiving the same mailing four times, each one addressed to slightly different recipients who are in fact the same person, (John Reid Esq, Mr J Read, Mr Johnny Reid, Mr J W Reed) is almost certain to put the recipient off in addition to being a costly flop for the sender. It is also fairly counterproductive to send a long letter to somebody asking them to take out your credit card, while in the same post they receive a dunning letter threatening them with legal proceedings if they don't pay up.

8. Plan repeat mailings well.

There can be all sorts of reasons why you get no response to a first mailing. It does not mean that you should cross the recipient off your list. It can however mean that you should change your tactics. Mailings should be seen as part of an ongoing campaign, not just a once-off, never-to-be-repeated effort. One very sophisticated company sends four mailings in every campaign to recipients who do not respond:

a. The initial mailer;
b. Second mailer with a further special offer;
c. Third mailer with a dramatic price reduction if returned in a very short time;
d. Final mailer with the original conditions (on the basis that one has spent so much on the prospect by this stage that he might as well pay the full price if he's going to buy at all).

CHAPTER 30

Advertising – The Law and the Code

We have talked about how to develop the most effective message for your advertising. But in doing so we have not touched at all upon the restrictions that are placed upon you.

These restrictions are not especially onerous and have the understandable aim of preventing obvious abuses. However it would be possible to make an honest mistake if one did not know precisely what is and what is not allowed.

The purpose of this chapter is to give a brief overview of the laws and codes that affect advertising. It can only be an overview. To give them all in detail would require a book of this length or longer. It should be emphasised that they are a combination of legal requirements and a voluntary code of practice, which in itself has evolved out of the voluntary, self-policing practices of various industries.

The central document that should be familiar to anybody producing advertising in Britain is the British Code of Advertising Practice (BCAP for short). This is an all-embracing code of self-control, administered by the advertisers, the advertising agencies, the media and their professional organisations, and dealing with all commercial advertisements other than those that are broadcast. For TV and radio commercials there is another code administered by the Independent Broadcasting Authority which is broadly congruent with the BCAP.

Any regular practitioner should have a copy of the latest codes at hand since this book's summary of their contents is no more than a brief guide. The IBA code is quite short (20 pages) while the BCAP extends to nearly 100 pages.

Generally, both codes are not hostile to advertising in any way, they simply aim to encourage advertising that is, in their own words, 'legal, decent, honest and truthful'. In case you think these four adjectives verge on the tautological, their different implications should be explained. 'Legal' means not in contravention of any law – if the Committee think an ad is against the law they will tell the complainant and encourage him to seek redress in that way. 'Decent' means not likely to cause widespread offence in matters of taste. 'Honest' appears to deal with the concept of dishonest and unethical intent – it catches the advertisement which, while not untruthful, has a blatantly misleading intention. 'Truthful' is a concept on which the code spends some seven pages. The burden of this is that advertising with facts, however tough, is to be welcomed provided that the facts, by the sophisticated *suggestio falsi* and the conscious *suppressio veri*, are not deliberately and intentionally distorted.

This is a reasonable provision and is fundamentally much better for the practice of advertising than the situation which exists in some countries where a comparative advertisement is simply not allowed whatever the facts of the case. Allowing any statement, as long as it is true, is essentially much more to the consumer's advantage.

The Code is, as has been said, self-policing. The advertising community bears the Code in mind constantly and aims to produce advertisements that observe its requirements. The media provide a second stage of defence since they have the right to reject any advertisement (and will, in some cases, reject advertisements that other media accept) and for them, the Code provides general standards of acceptability. However, so many advertisements are published every day that obviously complaints occur. The complaints are in the very nature of things most likely to come from your competitors, since they inevitably will feel that a particular claim discriminates against them. Objections can, of course come from the general public, but, in these cases, usually consist of specific pressure groups with objections to some particular industry.

The corollary of this is that individual industries develop accepted standards in their advertising. Each competitor knows what is tolerated and what goes too far.

The Code makes it clear that the advertiser has the ultimate responsibility for any statements made in advertisements and has the responsibility to substantiate any claim made. In the overall pursuit of truthfulness, the Code has a number of specific provisions.

It specifically allows recognisable exaggeration as a weapon of advertising provided there is no likelihood of consumers misunderstanding it.

It requires prices to featured in a way that avoids misunderstanding;

that is, usually VAT inclusive, the model shown to be the same as the model that is priced in large letters, for the price to include what one would normally expect to be included. It requires offers of items that are 'free' to be genuinely free and any extras to be clearly indicated. In the same way guarantees have to mean what they say. Switch selling (attracting enquiries with an extremely favourable offer which then proves to be sold out when anyone replies) is specifically prohibited.

The matter of fair representation is obviously a complex one, and the IBA Code has a paragraph that recognises the need for reproduction techniques that might be exaggerated in the flesh but give a correct impression on the television screen. Its requirement is that 'a fair and reasonable impression' must be conveyed.

The BCAP also requires testimonials to be fair and genuine and the permission of the testifier to be gained in advance.

There are also restrictions on exploiting the trademark or trade name of other businesses, unfairly denigrating other products and imitating other advertisements. (Though, in regard to the last point, the recognisable parody is a perfectly respectable weapon.)

This general part of the BCAP that affects all advertising is thus almost totally devoid of specific and detailed cavils. However, half the Code deals with the specifics of a few industries and types of business and is considerably more detailed.

The IBA Code has a few more specifics. It has, for instance, a number of products (in addition to a general ban on political, religious and charitable advertising) that are not allowed to advertise on the airwaves:

breath-testing devices;
matrimonial agencies;
fortune tellers;
undertakers;
employment services;
betting (including pools) and tipsters;
cigarettes;
private investigators;
advisory services for consumer or personal problems.

Then it has concerns that advertising should be always identifiable as advertising (shared to a certain extent by the BCAP, but they can rely on the media proprietors to be very conscious of this point) so it does not permit commercials to begin with the words 'News Flash' and has a specific provision against 'subliminal' advertising – a sign that the Code came into being during the period when Vance Packard's *The Hidden Persuaders* was a hot publishing property.

The law in relation to advertising is a very different kettle of fish. The laws that affect advertising in some way or other are legion but they all aim primarily to regulate specific businesses and trading practices and therefore have application to advertising only in so far as it is undertaken by those businesses. There is no law about advertising as such. But advertising is touched on, at least tangentially, in the following laws and regulations (to name only the more significant ones):

Advertisements (Hire Purchase) Act 1967
Consumer Credit Act 1974
Consumer Safety Act 1978
Consumer Transactions Order 1976
Fair Trading Act 1973
Food Labelling Regulations 1984
Gaming Act 1968
Income & Corporation Taxes Act 1970
Independent Broadcasting Authority Act 1973
Lotteries and Amusements Act 1976
Mail Order Transactions (Information) Order 1976
Medicines (Labelling and Advertising to the Public) Regulations 1978 (SI 41)
Misrepresentation Act 1976
Prevention of Corruption Acts 1889 to 1916
Price Marking (Bargain Offers) Order 1979
Sale of Goods Act 1979
Supply of Goods and Services Act 1982
Trade Descriptions Acts 1968 and 1972
Trading Stamps Act 1964
Unfair Contract Terms Act 1977
Unsolicited Goods and Services Act 1971
Weights & Measures Acts 1963, 1976

It would certainly be possible to spend a lifetime in advertising without even realising that many of these rules existed. Most only apply, as has been remarked, to particular businesses and types of trade. So it is much more easy to fall foul of the law if you are engaged in one of these trades.

In these special cases, detailed knowledge of the ins and outs of both Code and laws is vital. Many of the restrictions, while not, I think, in any case purely capricious, are not simply common sense. They need to be known.

What then are the businesses where both the law and the Codes have erected very specific regulations?

You should be informed as to the exact legal situation, and also as to the provisions of the two codes, if you are producing advertisements for any of the following:

a. Any medicinal product or any product using health claims

The regulations essentially prohibit selling direct to the public (and therefore advertising or labelling) medicines which claim to treat serious diseases including:

venereal disease
tuberculosis
cancer
diabetes
epilepsy or fits
kidney disease
paralysis
cataract
glaucoma
parasitic diseases
senility and degenerative conditions
any disease of the heart
hypertension

as well as treatments that deal with clinical, psychiatric or psychotic conditions, restoration of sexual potency, alleviation of chronic tiredness, rejuvenation, contraception (apart from via condoms and spermicides), fertility and infertility, addiction, insomnia, sedation, anaesthesia, regulation of menstrual flow.

In addition to these restrictions, the following cannot be advertised on radio or TV:

contraceptives
smoking cures
treatments for alcoholism
contact or corneal lenses
hair or scalp clinics
treatments for haemmorrhoids
pregnancy testing services
hypnosis, psychiatry etc.

The BCAP has three further broad areas of concern:

Impressions of professional advice or support. A series of restrictions which prevent any improper suggestion that a treatment enjoys a professional standing that it does not have. You may not refer to a 'college', 'hospital', 'clinic', 'institute' or 'laboratory' unless a properly supervised establishment actually exists. Similarly you may not make references to professional journals or doctors' opinions or prescribing habits, or the practice of hospitals unless they are fully substantiated.

The IBA Code further does not permit presenters to convey an impression of medical authority. Celebrities as presenters are also forbidden.

Particular claims. These include a general veto on the word 'cure' as against a claim to relieve symptoms, appeals to fear and exploitation of credulity, offers to diagnose conditions or treat them by post, and any activity militating against people seeking qualified medical advice.

The Code also prohibits the encouragement of excessive use of products, the making of exaggerated claims (particularly by using over-enthusiastic testimonials), offers to refund money and references to speed of absorption and so on that are not substantiated with appropriate evidence. Claiming that a product does not contain a particular ingredient in such a way as to suggest that this ingredient might be harmful is also prohibited.

Particular products. Those particular products singled out for special provisos are appliances for self treatment, hearing aids, height increase courses, non-allopathic medicines, pregnancy advisory services, sterilisation, vasectomy and pregnancy testing, rheumatic and allied conditions and smoking deterrent products.

Individual Treatments. The requirement is that such treatments do not appear to offer invariable success and that physically invasive treatments provide details of qualified personnel who will be responsible for treatment.

b. Hair and scalp products
These are treated very much as medicinal products in the demand for scientifically sound test evidence if any claim of effectiveness in

encouraging hair growth is made. Individual treatments such as hair transplantation are subject to the restrictions that the medicinal products code applies to physically invasive treatments.

c. Vitamins and minerals

This covers both medicinal products, and food and cosmetic products that also make vitamin and mineral claims.

If they are food products they are subject to the Food Labelling Regulations and this limits vitamin and mineral claims to the following:

Vitamins

Vitamin A

Thiamin (vitamin B^1)

Riboflavin (vitamin B^2)

Niacin

Folic Acid

Vitamin B^{12}

Vitamin C (ascorbic acid)

Vitamin D

Minerals

Calcium

Iodine

Iron

It also imposes regulations as to the amount of each substance that must be present to justify a claim.

The BCAP additionally restricts the selling of vitamins as a necessity for people enjoying a normal healthy diet and lists various situations in which vitamin deficiency may occur. The claims that vitamins speed recovery in convalescence and that they are of benefit in cosmetics require very specific substantiation.

d. Slimming products

Because of the wide number of differing slimming products and the careful checking such advertisements need, advertisers are asked to submit copy to media well before the planned publication date and to be most careful in distinguishing between different treatments. 'Figure control' products – ie corsets or exercise plans – should avoid giving the impression that they will produce weight loss. Both figure control and weight loss claims are not allowed for:

massage or vibrator machines
inflatable garments
sauna or Turkish baths
products based on osmosis
bath essences, soaps
products claiming artificially to increase the metabolic rate of the
   body
diuretics, laxatives
products and methods claiming to offer 'spot reduction' (ie to
   remove fats from specific parts of the body)
products and methods claiming to achieve slimming through the
   removal of 'cellulite'.

Other restrictions on slimming products include: a prohibition of claims of specific weight or inch loss or efficacy within a specific period or testimonials that tend in that direction, together with claims of infallibility or dramatic differences from other slimming products. Claims referring to 'obesity' are also prohibited together with claims that specific ingredients in themselves hasten weight loss, that temporary weight loss through the loss of water from the body is a method of slimming or anything that encourages unwise dieting without due attention to medical advice — 'crash' diets are *expressis verbis* forbidden.

e. Cosmetics

The cosmetic field is only a difficult one if its claims get out of the cosmetic area into the general areas of health — restrictions are on claims about the prevention of ageing and on claims of specific physiological or biological effects. Those restrictions already noted affecting vitamins and minerals, hair and scalp products and cosmetic surgery do of course apply.

f. Financial services

In this rapidly growing field, the effect of the restrictions is to oblige the advertiser to explain fully the possible consequences of any particular features of the product advertised. For instance, he must make it clear that illustrations from the past are not necessarily guides to the future, what assumptions underlie the promise of tax benefits, what effect withdrawal of capital will have, that investments which are not guaranteed can go down as well as up.

The IBA Code prohibits the sale of financial products 'off the

193

screen' and also does not allow well-known presenters to 'lend their authority' to any investment opportunity offered.

In cases where credit is offered this is subject to the provisions of the Consumer Credit Act 1974 and the regulations that accompany it.

g. Offers of employment

All situations vacant should be genuine vacancies and should not require readers to send money for further details. Offers of vocational training should not make unconditional promises of future employment. Homeworker schemes should not overestimate the realistic earnings potential, should specify any charges to be made, should describe the work adequately. Business opportunities should be clearly identified as such and not presented as a form of paid employment.

h. 'Collectibles'

Under this heading are to be understood all limited editions of items offered typically through mail order. The restrictions aim to inhibit claims that overstate the investment potential of such goods and lack of clarity in the nature of the limitation imposed on numbers.

i. Cigarettes

This category, which also includes cigarette components and hand-rolling tobacco, is the outcome of discussions between the Department of Health and Social Security, the Advertising Standards Authority and the Tobacco Industry. It has been in place since 1975.

Its restrictions are such as to eliminate many of the traditional ways of advertising cigarette brands and to lead to a form of advertising which simply aims to achieve brand identification. It specifically forbids:

persuading people to start smoking
addressing the young in any way
encouraging heavy smoking
suggesting that smoking demonstrates manliness or feminine charm
using testimonials from celebrities or members of particular callings or groups engaged in activities which excite admiration
connecting smoking with sexual, social or business success or with sport.

No advertising for products of this type is allowed on TV or radio.

j. Alcoholic drinks

The advertising for alcoholic drinks is not subject to anywhere near such tight restrictions as cigarettes but the code of the industry tends obviously in the same broad direction – the limitation of heavy consumption and appeals to the young. It also discourages appeals to social, business or sexual success, and any associations between alcoholic drinks and driving or using dangerous machinery – though warnings of danger may be used in advertising.

Drink advertising cannot emphasise any health aspects or boast of alcoholic strength, or issue challenges to try any particular drink. In broadcast media it must further desist from any competitions.

Alcoholic drinks are also subject to the Food Labelling Regulations mentioned below.

k. Food

The BCAP and the IBA Code do not treat foods as a special category except in so far as they make vitamin or slimming claims. The Food Labelling Regulations should be familiar to every food manufacturer for his formulation and labelling. They also apply to advertising. They limit (but do not generally prohibit) claims using words such as the following to products that fulfil certain criteria of formulation, preparation or origin:

butter
cream
dietary or dietetic
fresh, garden, green
milk
starch-reduced
alcohol-free
dealcoholised, non-alcoholic
shandy
sweetened liqueur
tonic wine
vintage
Scotch Whisky.

In addition to these specific rules applying to particular categories, the BCAP contains a number of guidelines in the depiction of children in advertisements and the advertising of products addressed to children. The IBA Code has all the same provisos and several more of its own.

The first group of rules seeks to discourage ads that, by example, might encourage children to do something dangerous. It prohibits depicting children unattended in the street, driving or riding on agricultural machines, leaning out of high windows, reaching to take things from high shelves, using matches or electrical appliances and so on.

The IBA Code also requires children depicted in commercials to be 'reasonably well-mannered and well-behaved'.

The second aims to stop advertisers exploiting children as customers. It enjoins naming the price of the advertised product, not exaggerating the results of use of the product or making it hard to judge the product's true size, and discourages appeals to buy based on loyalty or popularity among peers. Children must not appear as presenters nor as formal testimonial-givers. The codes also prohibit anything that might encourage children to pester their parents to buy – hence the demise of that winsome youngster who pleaded (albeit without actually opening his mouth) 'Don't forget the fruit gums, Mum.'

In addition to these restrictions on content, the IBA Code also has a large group of products that may not be advertised at times when children may be expected to be in the audience – usually arbitrarily taken to be before nine pm.

We have not made any comment about the various restrictions on the offering of mail order products here. There is a sizeable chapter of the Code devoted to them and, in addition, media usually make specific rules and conditions. Further, the law in the form of such statutes as the Mail Order Transactions (Information) Order 1976, the Hallmarking Act 1973, the Consumer Safety Act 1978 and the Post Office Act 1953 has various things to say. For all these reasons, mail order advertisers are advised to acquaint themselves with the requirements of all statutes and restrictions in their originals.

CHAPTER 31

How to Know
a Good Idea

Advertising agencies play very unfairly with their clients. Let me explain why. They sit on a briefing for months, they develop a lot of varied answers to the problems it poses, they discuss them and refine them, they produce layouts and storyboards, and they then present these with all the showmanship they can muster.

None of this is unfair. What is unfair is that the company which has hired the agency is expected to make an instant comment and then does it usually through the mouth of a young product manager whose total business experience may be three or four years at most.

Agencies plan their presentations with the understandable aim of success. It is hard to make money on preparing advertising if you are unable to sell your ideas and have to go back constantly and revise. It is also arguable that the client gets the second best idea the second time around, the third best the third time around and so on. The problem is that, because the acceptance process is tense and immediate and allows little time for reconsideration, one of two things may happen, both bad. The company may buy a thoroughly bad campaign presented slickly and with bravura, or the company may fail to recognise a piece of brilliance that could have made a dramatic difference to its sales.

Appreciating what advertising is all about when it is in the rough stage is not an easy job. It calls for an ability to envisage the finished ad and commercial behind the layout, and it requires the ability to look at these things like a detached – not to say uninterested – consumer. Neither talent is inborn. Some people (who may well make excellent product managers because of their logical, numerate minds and their clarity in self expression) are often almost totally devoid of the sensitivity or detachment that is required.

Companies often try to deal with this by giving their young product managers checklists of points to look for. More sophisticated than most, Beavan Ennis of Ennis Associates of New York (a management training company that runs a highly respected series of courses for brand managers) has developed the checklists reproduced here. They are more detailed than most and divide the process up into a number of vital steps which we will consider separately.

EVALUATING ADVERTISING
Initial considerations

- The first step in the evaluation process is to be sure the advertising meets the requirements of the copy strategy. There is no need to proceed further if the suggested advertising is not on strategy.
- If there are doubts about whether it is or is not on strategy, ask the agency to relate the strategy to the proposed campaign.
- Avoid suggested changes in the strategy based solely on executional considerations.

The first consideration has to be: Is the advertising on strategy? If this cannot be answered affirmatively, forget the rest! Ask the agency to explain the connection if the advertising is not obviously on strategy rather than jumping unhesitatingly into making a judgement yourself.

The Second Step

1. Assess the *creative* qualities of the advertising, in terms of its
   - selling values
   - communication values

2. Assess the construction qualities of the advertising

It is also important to distinguish between those factors that concern the company *vitally*, the ability of the advertising to sell and to communicate, and those factors that are logically more in the agency's area of expertise. The implication is that the product manager or whoever is evaluating the advertising has to take the first group of values much more seriously than the second. The Ennis evaluation system goes on to give these guidelines for evaluating selling values and communication values:

The selling values

What to look for	*How to evaluate it*
1. Basic campaign idea	Does it translate the positioning concept? Is it meaningful to the consumer? Does it have long-term potential?
2. Support or benefit	Is it believable? Is it obvious or should it be demonstrated?
3. Action-oriented	Will it stimulate consumers to try the product? Is it motivating?
4. Recall	Is it memorable? Distinctive from competition?

The communication values

What to look for	*How to evaluate it*
1. Clarity	Is it simple? Does it look 'busy'? Are there any extraneous ideas in it?
2. Flow	Is it logical? Do the ideas fall in their natural sequence? Is it hard to follow?
3. Interest	How different is the executional approach from the competition?
4. Visual relevance	Does the illustration tie in with the main campaign idea? Does it communicate the positioning concept or act as a lead-in to it?

Apart from these essentials, the construction qualities of the advertising should also be looked at, and the Ennis system gives the following suggestions for these

Construction qualities

All advertising:
  Is the product properly identified?
  Are its use/benefits quickly established?

> TV advertising:
> Are the audio and visual tracks compatible?
> Are the claims distinctive?
>
> Print advertising:
> Do the headline and illustration work together?
> Does the copy layout reflect the normal eye flow?

Now this system is undoubtedly a solid one for all who have to evaluate advertising to use. The real benefit of such checklists is that they concentrate the mind on those factors which are important. This is an important service since, if this is not done, the initial reaction may dwell on trivialities and the whole discussion may centre round the exact expression on somebody's face or the precise colour of the background.

The single most important thing (to risk a repetition that cannot be repeated enough!) is that the strategy is communicated. If it is not, do not waste time trying to reconstruct the advertising there and then so that the strategy can be shoe-horned in – go back to the drawing board.

Once one is satisfied that the strategy is communicated, then the criteria listed above which make for effective selling and effective communication need to be considered, and finally the elements of solid workmanlike construction.

This careful and logical consideration is very positive – subject to one proviso.

This proviso consists of what has variously been called 'the gulp factor', the 'boiing system' and the 'hackles' system. What these all mean is that the ideal, powerful, perfect solution should make you gulp when you see it, should make something go 'boiing', or should cause the hackles on your neck to rise. Really great advertising has a blinding simplicity about it. You come across the perfect answer and ask yourself 'Why hasn't anybody thought of it before?' Sometimes it is so blindingly obvious that you simply don't believe it is actually a new idea.

For many years I had a quotation from W H Auden on my office wall which said, 'The greatest writer cannot see through a brick wall, but, unlike the rest of us, he does not build one.' Young copywriters suspected that I was trying to tell them something (and were right) but in many cases did not quite understand what. What I was actually trying to say is that we often introduce unneccessary complication and then further complication trying to explain the complication we have already introduced. The answer, of course, is not to introduce any in the first place.

The 'gulp', 'boiing' or 'hackles' systems are difficult ones for clients to apply. But they should always be applied and applied first by the creative people attempting to produce the advertising. If it cannot excite you, it is unlikely to excite anyone else. If it cannot excite the reader then it is unlikely to get him to read and absorb.

Some creative people of course rely on boiings and hackles and gulps too much. It is important to realise that such insights – where you suddenly 'see' the whole ad or the whole commercial before you and only have to write it down – in nine cases out of ten do require some detailed work. The brilliant painting that the artist sees in one blinding flash will still need a lot of careful work in those areas that are conveniently muzzy at the moment of conception, the brilliant sonnet will be there in essence but to get its rhyme scheme right and its scansion perfect may take hours of work. In such cases, it is always well to remember that your client may well be looking at the thing with some such checklist as those we have quoted in his hand. So do his work for him. Go through these requirements critically and seriously. If you have a really outstanding piece of advertising then it will come through with flying colours. And the exercise of having done it – and probably of having introduced some small amendments and excisions and amplifications – will only make the subsequent sale all the easier.

CHAPTER 32

When and How to Use Research

One of the clichés of the advertising business is the ongoing conflict that is supposed to exist between the creative function and that of research. It is a cliché that, in my experience, has a certain truth as its foundation but also some fairly fundamental misconceptions.

All marketing research (of which advertising research forms a part) is essentially directed towards making the marketing operation more effective. It attempts to do this by giving the marketing management some facts to base its decisions on rather than personal impressions and opinions. It uses a large number of differing techniques, some of which seem intimidatingly scientific. However this should not blind one to the truth that most research falls into one of two categories.

Either it aims to forecast what will happen – in which case its function is predictive. Or it aims to record and interpret what has already happened – in which case its function is historical.

Now, no competent researcher would suggest that the accuracy that can typically be achieved in the first of these functions is in any way comparable with that which can emerge from the second. Unfortunately managers, who do not perhaps always appreciate the fundamental differences between the two functions, often act as if both are equally trustworthy – simply because they are both called 'research'.

Marketing management is a heavy user of research and seeks the answers to a number of different questions.

First there are questions of consumer behaviour. How many people of what age, sex, geographical location or socio-economic group form the market for a particular product category? What needs and desires do they expect such a product to fulfil? What products do they buy at the moment, in what quantities, at what sort of shops, in what frequency and at what price?

These questions are all more or less factual. And they are all historical. By quantified studies of consumers and by store audits such as Nielsen these questions can be answered historically with an impressive degree of accuracy. The only group of questions for which it is sometimes hard to get reliable answers is the one dealing with needs and desires. Sometimes people's needs are hard for them to verbalise, particularly if the need is of a psychological nature. People will not usually say, 'I smoke such and such a cigarette because it helps me compensate for feelings of inadequacy.' However projective techniques can usually give one a good guess at least at such subterranean motivations.

The whole thing becomes considerably more difficult when we attempt to project such questions into the future and predict future consumer behaviour. Questions like, 'Would you buy a product that did such-and-such?' are very easy to answer positively (and most people do so because they like to be helpful) but it is clear that such answers are not to be regarded as very solid until a product that actually does such-and-such is offered to them. Even then, the fundamental willingness to be interested that a positive answer may imply can be strongly affected by how well the product is perceived to do the job it claims to do, its price, its name, all its other image components and – very far from least – all the other things that may have happened in the marketplace in the year or so that elapsed since you asked the question.

The things that management needs to know to produce effective advertising are all, unfortunately, in the predictive area. Here, we take the factual knowledge we have of what people buy today and the reasonably accurate picture we have of today's motivations and attempt to guess what might happen when we put a new product or a new advertising stimulus into this situation. Clearly we cannot say with precision what will happen, and the consumers themselves are probably no better able to say so. Additionally, whereas it is quite easy for consumers to tell you with accuracy what products they have bought, they are far less aware of which advertisements have influenced them and very unsure which advertisements might influence them in some hypothetical future.

Added to these difficulties are the results of a pressure to save both time and money. Ideally you need to know if your positioning and copy strategy are right, if your execution idea is arresting, if your ad is noticeable and memorable before you spend a lot of money on it in the media and even before you spend money on producing it. (If a 30 second TV spot costs £30,000 to film then the decision to junk it is not very

203

easily taken.) Yet inevitably research that attempts to make such bold leaps into the future is bound to be less reliable than research that deals with the final advertisement in the real media situation.

People who create advertisements are people whose instinct is to think intuitively. They certainly do not neglect the importance of facts or product knowledge, but they are not always trained or inclined to gather such knowledge from statistical tables. They often regard the researcher's models of the market as extremely simplistic (which of course they are – their whole aim is to make a complex and shifting mass of motivations visible and understandable by simplifying them).

Additionally it must be understood that creating advertisements is essentially an artistic activity. It requires commitment, creativity, enthusiasm and belief in what you are doing.

If someone essentially uninvolved criticises and dissects your brainchild soon after its birth, your instinct, rightly or wrongly, is to rush to its protection.

Between the scepticism of the ad makers, the demand of marketers for facts and measurements, and the cautious response of the researchers that they can only measure part of the problem and make projections that may or may not stand up, an armoury of rough-and-ready research techniques that go some way to dealing with the difficulties has been assembled. Nobody pretends they are perfect. But within the constraints of time, money, simplicity, and speed they go some way to answering some of the basic problems.

There are three points that need to be made about any advertising research:

1. Since so much of its conclusions are about matters which are in the final analysis subjective, it always needs to be interpreted carefully and undogmatically.

2. Since costs tend to keep sample size down, differences of one and two per cent will often reflect the opinions of one or two people – only quite large numerical differences are really significant.

3. One develops a feel for a particular technique if it is used frequently, and reliability is increased if one has a growing bank of historical data behind one. This is vitiated if one experiments with every technique around and does not use one or two consistently.

With these warnings let us consider some of the research techniques that are commonly used in marketing to help produce and evaluate advertising.

Group interviews

A round-table discussion on a generalised subject (like 'shaving' if you are thinking of introducing a new shaving soap) is held with between six and twelve typical consumers. The idea is to get broad insights into attitudes, needs and wishes. They can be stimulating and very valuable and they have the advantages of being low in cost and speedy to set up. *Cautions*: A professional moderator is very desirable, as is a series of groups rather than just one. Groups can only suggest points that then usually need verifying in larger-scale research – it is fatal to assume that because three people out of a group of six say something that 50 per cent of your target market is of that opinion.

Usage and attitude studies

These are fairly complex, statistically reliable studies of particular markets carried out perhaps every five years or so. They will typically provide a complete demographic picture of users and potential users and the products they prefer, attitudes towards products, frequency of purchase and intensity of use and the benefits sought, including points of satisfaction and dissatisfaction. *Cautions*: Very desirable as a benchmark for any company planning to do business in a market, such studies are inevitably costly and time-consuming so that in fast-moving markets, during the time elapsed between pilot study planning and completion of the final study the market may well have changed significantly.

Brand mapping studies

These are studies measuring the opinions of consumers about brands on a series of attributes. They are carried out in personal interviews with large, statistically reliable samples. They could of course be incorporated into a usage and attitude study. *Cautions*: One needs to know the relative importance of the attributes measured to get any value from such studies.

Product tests

These are primarily designed to test the acceptability of a new product, but often have implications for advertising. The product is placed in a sample of homes (usually quite a small sample) either on its own (a so-called monadic test) or in company with a major competitor (if both products are packaged anonymously this is a so-called blind test). After an appropriate period users are asked their opinions, asked to rate various characteristics and state their buying intentions, expected price and so on. *Cautions*: In blind tests products must be equally fresh and of equal quality otherwise the test product can enjoy a deceptive advantage, coming straight from the factory whereas the competitor comes through the trade channel. In monadic tests, consumers are often eager to speak well of a product they have received free and this must be allowed for.

A variant on the product test is to pack the same product in two different packages with two different brand names and ask people to compare them. Since the products themselves are identical any differences must be due to the name, package design and general image – an ingenious way to measure the effect of these dimensions.

Advertisement pre-tests

Usually carried out in personal interviews or in small groups, rough advertisements are shown to consumers and their opinions on key elements – picture, headline etc – are sought. *Cautions*: Quite quick and cheap, their small scale makes them unreliable as a guide to the relative importance of different appeals, but of value if they are only asked to evaluate how well various executions transmit a particular appeal. Since the ads are usually in rough form, it is always difficult to assess what influence the unfinished nature of the ads has had.

TV commercial pre-tests

In these tests small groups of people are invited to a viewing theatre and they see a short programme with commercials integrated into it, the commercials usually being, for cost reasons, in an unfinished form – either inexpensive films or roughly animated storyboards (so-called 'animatics'). Since the commercials other than the one being tested are used again and again and have known attention values, the test commercial can also be reasonably reliably measured in regard to the viewers' ability to remember it. It is then often shown a second time and detailed questions about attitudes and understanding are asked. *Cautions*: Most kinds of rough commercials vary drastically from the finished commercial, and unfortunately to greatly varying degrees. This may favour one interpretation at the expense of another. Also the danger of making strategic decisions on what is exclusively an executional test, as mentioned in advertisement pre-tests, must be constantly guarded against.

TV recall studies

In these studies a finished commercial is transmitted normally and a sample of viewers – typically around 100 who were viewing at the time the commercial was transmitted – is asked what they remember and what they think. Telephone interviews are the norm because of the need to talk to a large number of people within a limited period (usually 24 hours). *Cautions*: While very valuable as a measure of attention values, recall cannot do much to measure persuasiveness. High attention may result from a high irritation factor. Recall has also been tried for radio commercials (where the in-and-out nature of the radio audience makes the compilation of sensible statistics nearly impossible) and for print ads (where overall lower recall levels lead to confusion with other ads for the same brand) but is only used in an important way for TV.

Reading and noting (Starch) studies

These studies constituted some of the earliest advertising research ever carried out and have been responsible for producing much of the basic knowledge we have of factors influencing attention and reading. Personal interviewers would take a recent issue of a popular magazine round to a number of households and go through it page by page, asking the respondent if each particular ad had been noted, if the brand name had been registered, if most of the copy had been read. The results for each individual ad are limited to these three simple measurements, but obviously anyone using the technique for his own ad exclusively can add other questions. *Cautions*: The technique is very inexpensive per ad if applied to a complete magazine and the information that is built up over a period is considerable. However the method is comparatively crude and subtle differences between ads are not usually registered.

Commercial tracking studies

These are comparatively large-scale studies conducted often by telephone with the aim of measuring the awareness of the (predominantly TV) advertising of a number of brands all in the same market. Information is usually limited to simple measures such as the brand name, the key visual, the claim and is sometimes tied to a statement of buying intention. *Cautions*: Very much a measure that tells you where you stand today and which needs to be repeated to give any useful actionable information. It can usually only be applied to oligopolistic markets in which the brands are all large, well-known and seen as broadly similar. There, as a continuous measure of how the race is going it is fascinating – but not very deep. It never tells you *why* you're not doing as well as your competitor.

Concealed offer ad tests

These tests are only used for advertisements and are quite rapid and cheap. The advertisement is inserted in a suitable magazine or newspaper and an offer of a free sample (or if that is not suitable, a free booklet or a price-off voucher) is built into the copy. (It is not usually the subject of a coupon since there are a number of people who are dedicated coupon-clippers and the aim is to identify the effect of the ad, not to attract the greatest response to the offer.) The assumption is that someone who sends in for the offer has both read the ad to the end and found it convincing. Used on a consistent basis it enables a backlog of information to be built up as to which of a number of subjects produce the best results. *Cautions*: Can only be used for press ads and does have the problem that a money-saving offer is not the same as a full-price purchase.

Test markets

These are very costly and complex operations in which a product is marketed in a limited area of the country (usually a TV area) and this whole area is carefully measured in terms of sales result. Detailed attitudinal research may also be carried out in the area. *Cautions*: Because by definition the entire marketing mix is being employed in the area, a test market can only be a test of a particular advertising approach if different copy to the rest of the country or to another comparable area is employed. A corollary of this is that the results are often not readable – the marginal differences in sales level being ascribable to the subtle but important differences that inevitably occur from one area to another – different consumer attitudes, different power dispositions in the trade, different demographics, and so on.

When do you use what?

Very simply which technique you use to answer which sort of question can be summed up as follows:

Basic consumer positioning
Group interviews followed by statistically reliable attitude study. Product test or brand mapping study helpful as back-up.

Defining basic advertising ideas
Advertisement pre-tests in group interviews, refined by larger-scale testing of finished ads/commercials in theatre tests and Starch tests.

Measuring attention and interest
Starch tests, TV pre-tests, recall studies.

Measuring willingness to buy
Concealed offer tests, area market tests.

Measuring campaign penetration against competitors
Commercial tracking studies, TV recall studies (if comparative data available).

Measuring overall effectiveness
Market test.

How do you use research?

The key to using research constructively is not to treat it as some unquestionable gospel but as a useful if fairly inexact tool.
Be sure to remember:

a. Treat the numbers with reserve. If the differences are not large then one score is probably not much better than another.

b. The 'verbatims' – the actual words in which people described the ad – should be read with real interest. Look for evidence of involvement, concern, interest, identification. Look for people remembering the little details that show they really absorbed the whole thing.

c. Make sure you understand how a research score comes about. If attention is low then it is probably the headline that needs sharpening up in an ad, the basic situation which is uninvolving in a commercial. If a claim is poorly recalled then it is either not dealing with an issue people identify with or the words are not challenging and interesting. Research can help you make useful fixes – but only if you learn to understand what it is trying to tell you.

PART FIVE

Planning to Get the Most for Your Money

CHAPTER 33

How to Prepare a Budget

This book has concentrated on the creative task of preparing advertising and given the business of marketing, to which it is closely connected, not much more than an occasional sideways glance.

The major activity in formal marketing centres round the preparation of an annual budget and marketing plan. These two are usually very closely linked, the budget being a statement of how much one plans to sell, how much needs to be spent to achieve those sales and, finally, how much profit will result. The marketing plan shows how the money appropriated for marketing activities will be spent – how much on advertising, how much on promotions, how much on PR, how much on other selling activities. The formal selling organisation, the sales force, sometimes falls within the scope of the product's marketing plan, but more often, since it sells all products the company produces, it is simply part of the overhead that the product manager is required to accommodate, just like the rent on the factory and the workers' social club.

It is obviously not possible to carry out advertising activities without some broad guidelines as to the funds available. Certain media require a reasonably large budget or their use is impossible or impractical. And, since the ultimate aim of all marketing activity is to earn profits, it is unrealistic to look at advertising without paying some attention to the practices of budgeting.

Five methods of defining the advertising budget

Apart from the 'TON' method ('think of a number'), there are five ways in which advertising budgets can be determined.

Spending per case
This simply takes the planned sales for the coming year and allocates a certain sum for each statistical unit (usually a case or outer, but it could

equally well be a barrel, a tonne or whatever unit the industry reckons in) to advertising and promotion. During the year the sum spent is reconciled to the sales actually achieved with the aim of coming out more or less right at year's end.

Advantages and disadvantages: The method cannot drive you into bankruptcy and it does guarantee that successful brands get expenditure that reflects their success, rather than being raided to pay for less successful products. However it can make it very hard to get out of a downward trend.

Industry/company sales percentage
This method takes the individual brand case rate and substitutes for it an industry-wide or company-wide average.

Advantages and disadvantages: It has the simplicity and reality of the case rate method and often similar disadvantages. It also has the problem that there is no incentive for a brand to achieve a premium price so as to be able to promote at a higher level than the market as a whole.

Competitive parity
Under this system, a brand simply aims to equal the expenditure of a particular competitor or (amounting to the same thing) to achieve an equivalent share of media voice.

Advantages and disadvantages: One problem of this method is that the target one is focusing on is always a year out of date. A further problem in viability can occur if one simply fails to come anywhere close to the target competitor in terms of sales, or if your company's costs are higher than theirs.

Historical spending
This method simply projects last year's spending into this year.

Advantages and disadvantages: You can hardly expect to grow if you continue spending the same.

Task method
This method starts out by estimating marketing requirements and then tots up the bill. This is then the budget.

Advantages and disadvantages While it seems far and away the best method since it relates spending to what one plans to achieve, this method has a nasty tendency to be totally unaffordable. What a brand 'really needs to spend' is often larger than its entire sales income.

It will be seen that all methods have serious flaws and this is probably why very few companies ever employ a particular method to the exclusion of all others. The most reasonable way of setting the budget is probably a combination of various methods – and the way suggested here is probably broadly in line with many companies' practices.

Recommended method for defining the advertising budget

1. Make a preliminary sales forecast
This will always be a part historical, part rule-of-thumb game. It is a matter of guessing the future when a lot of the factors that will influence the future are still unknown.

There are some useful guidelines, however:

a. *Forecast in units.* Because you are aiming to get a budget as the result of your forecasting it is tempting to forecast in money terms. This is a sure way to get a poor result. Always look at your unit sales (and don't forget to distinguish between units sold at normal price and units sold at discounted promotional prices) before converting them into money.

b. *Use at least three years' sales as a base.* When I talk of three years' sales, I am assuming you have a product with fairly high frequency of purchase. If you are looking at a high ticket item with a purchase rhythm of five or six years or more, then you need to look back even further.

c. *Look very closely at recent trends.* If you can isolate why the sales in the last few months have not been what you might have expected from the last two or three years, then you stand a good chance of spotting whatever it is that will make your forecast turn sour.

d. *Look at – and attempt to forecast – market changes.* Make realistic allowances for your competitors being at least as active as you intend to be. Far too much forecasting is done on the unreal basis that everybody else will be frozen into inactivity.

e. *Follow seasonality but discard aberrations.* Your analysis of the previous years will show that there are certain oddities that can be explained away one way or other. Do not make the mistake of including these in your forecast. Seasonal patterns that repeat year for year (and they often occur even though the product may not logically be seasonal) should always be reflected.

2. Turn the unit forecast into a sensible financial forecast
This involves taking the units and converting them into money by applying a realistic selling price to them. Here the danger of overestimating is considerable if you:

a. simply assume your list selling price. At the very least you should know what average price you actually achieved last year and project a similar price forward, amended for inflation.

b. neglect to allow for price-off, promotional expenditure depressing your average selling price.

c. neglect to allow for the effect of large customers (whom you may be expecting to take more product) insisting on a lower overall price in recognition of this.

3. Relate the forecast to the funds produced
This simply means applying the case rate principle to determine what total money you could produce, even if you made no profit at all, on the basis of the forecast you have produced. The sum looks like this:

Sales	100%
Cost of goods	32%
Margin	68%
Overhead costs	12%
Available for marketing and profit	56%

In other words, you now know that you could spend 56 per cent of your sales income on marketing the product without actually costing the company money (but without making any either!). Assuming that the company expects you to make, say, 20 per cent profit you know that, on the standard calculation, you would have 36 per cent for marketing and advertising.

4. Consider the costs of marketing objectives
Now you lay your calculations aside for a moment and look at your overall marketing objectives. Suppose you intend to increase share of market in the coming year – then pencil in a budget to achieve this and

relate it to the 36-56 per cent spread you have already defined. This is the task method – but without the 'blue sky' component that tends to drive it into the stratosphere.

You are certainly heading for disaster if you assume that your selling costs can be contained within last year's parameters. What, for instance, has been the history of media costs in the media you use? Pencil in a reasonable sum for media inflation. Some rate increases may already be announced. It is probably safe to say that those who have not made an announcement yet will follow suit.

5. Consider the possibilities of increasing sales and expenditure
Suppose you feel that your advertising is working very well and that you could considerably increase sales if you increased advertising. (Let me say that I think such a potentiality would be more tenable if backed by a limited area test in the current year rather than just a gut feel.) Then, for this or some similar reason, you may feel able to increase the budgeted sales figure if you take a compensating increase of advertising budget into account.

6. Amend your recommended budget in the light of this
Let us assume that after accounting for increased selling costs but also allowing for some investment spending and the increased sales it will produce, you come up with a recommended budget that is about 44 per cent of the total income available for marketing and for profit.

7. Consider competitive activities
Now is the time to relate your budget of 44 per cent to what your main competitor spent last year. This could show that you are still going to be apparently heavily outspent. Or alternatively it may suggest that you could actually cut back. Let us assume that your competitor spent slightly more than the money you would have available, but you believe you have more efficient advertising with higher attention values, so can reasonably challenge him with a budget of the level indicated.

8. Reconcile product aims with overall company aims
What now follows is a complex piece of horse-trading in which the representative of a particular product does not have the only or even perhaps the loudest voice. The product manager will recommend a certain budget (perhaps the 44 per cent we posited). It may well be amended downwards to accommodate company profit objectives and it is also I suppose theoretically possible for management to amend it

upwards. Obviously the product manager with the best argued case is most likely to get something approaching the budget he wants. The reaction of management is always likely to be guided by what long-term goals they have for the particular product concerned and where it stands in a hierarchy of priorities. It is hard to advocate very heavy spending and low profit levels for a product that you have decided should be 'milked' while it is in a long, terminal decline. On the other hand, a product that obviously represents the business of the future can very easily be given the go-ahead to spend its full earnings and return no profit, if it is obviously correct to seek to establish a strong position in the market.

CHAPTER 34

The Marketing and Advertising Plan

As explained in the last chapter, the formal marketing plan is the central business planning instrument used by most companies that market consumer goods. Preparing it, selling it, updating it and carrying it out is the main responsibility of the product manager.

In so far as the reader of this book is a product manager he will not need it to tell him how to prepare a plan – it will be constantly impressed on him as a major part of his job. However, there are other people in smaller businesses and in industrial firms and financial and service institutions who may not work to the discipline of an annual plan and may well welcome a brief indication as to how it is best done. The actual form of marketing plans is extremely simple and condensed – and it is a very useful discipline even for a one-man firm to have one. Companies that use advertising as a marketing tool can benefit particularly from a clear and formalised understanding of their aims and intentions.

The exact form of the annual marketing plan varies from company to company. The scheme I shall be putting forward is however typical of that used in most consumer goods companies, who have the most experience and sophistication in using this tool. Increasingly, other businesses are coming to use similar plans. It is important to realise that it is a practical working tool. The product's success or failure is defined by it and it should be constantly updated through the year and actual performance against the plan should be constantly under review.

It may seem that this kind of 'plan tyranny' is counterproductive and leaves management no time to manage. In fact the opposite is true. If marketing planning does not take place, if strategies are not worked out and adhered to, then each day is an *ad hoc* attack on the unknown. The field of advertising is one where planning is particularly necessary because advertising presupposes, as we have seen, slowly and deliberately building a clear positioning and an awareness of it. This can only happen if long-term thinking is the rule.

The components of the marketing plan

The actual planning sections of the Marketing Plan will usually be contained under three headings:

1. Objectives
2. Strategies
3. Plans.

One problem of novice plans is that these three distinct concepts tend to become confused one with the other. We will treat them separately and in a little detail.

Objectives
Objectives are usually *financial* – a certain sales volume at a certain price producing a certain profit.

To achieve this, certain subsidiary objectives (for the purpose of simplicity we employ the word 'goals') which are not financial will also need to be achieved – a particular share of market, a particular distribution level, perhaps a target awareness level. These goals, while legitimate and important, do not take the place of the fundamental financial target which is the objective of the marketing activity.

Strategies
These are the broad methods employed to achieve the financial objective. There will be a strategy for each component part of the overall marketing activity – ie a copy strategy that defines what the product will attempt to communicate, a media strategy that will define which media will be used in this communication, a promotion strategy, if promotion is an important part of the marketing mix, that will define the promotional route to be employed and the sums that that will take. The goals referred to above are usually part of the component strategies. The goal of the copy strategy might be to achieve a prompted awareness of a certain level. The media strategy might have the goal of achieving a certain reach and frequency within a defined audience.

Plans
These are simply the detailed forms of the strategies above. If the

activities are not too broad, then the strategy statement can also be immediately complemented and explained by its plan. It is only with large brands with a large number of different promotions, special campaigns and test campaigns, national copy and test market copy that the divorce of strategy and plan serves a valid purpose.

Function of the plan

Writing a clear plan is an excellent exercise even if you are a one-man firm. The simple discipline of putting things down on paper forces you to put numbers on your aims, to think your objectives through, to have a real strategy rather than just pious hopes.

However, with this proviso, the real purpose of plans is to facilitate organised management in comparatively large businesses. The function of a plan here – in addition to all the good things we have mentioned above, which benefit the author of the plan – is to make sure that the total management team know what they're about. It also helps to have clear objectives and a clear strategy for reaching them, because only so can you say, at the end of the year, 'Yes, we have succeeded' or 'No, we haven't made it'.

It is a function of this wider purpose, where the plan is the document that sums up everything that this particular product is going to do in the coming fiscal year, that the plan be complete. It should give management a complete, easily-followed, unequivocal guide to what is being targeted. It should also, while not giving any excess information, give all the key information that makes it possible to judge if the objectives aimed at are reasonable and the strategy sound.

Obviously this function demands a carefully written, very condensed plan with a clear structure. How should such a structure appear?

Form of the plan

The plan will usually have a form on the following lines:

- Objective(s)
- Background data and analysis of the market and the prospects for the brand.
- Goals and strategies
  - copy
  - media
  - promotion
- Plans for each activity with financial summaries.

Much like a news story, the marketing plan starts at the end with the sales achieved and the profit produced. It then goes deeper and deeper into how this is all going to happen. The reason for this structure is that management then only needs to read further if they are not sure of the measure proposed. If they are in agreement they do not need to go into the detail.

Writing the plan
Marketing plans are not literary exercises. They should be clear, factual and devoid of personal bias. They should avoid editorial comment and ideally support every assertion with facts. While comparatively few of us are so well supplied with facts from research that we can avoid doing quite a sizable amount of 'guesstimating', it is still a useful discipline to put estimates in numerical terms. A weakness in marketing planning is a feature of most smaller businesses and nowhere is this more evident than in their failure to quantify their aims and strategies. Getting the habit of thinking in numbers forces one to think precisely – and also makes you aware of the information that you do not have.

An effective plan requires a clear understanding of the market, what is happening that will make the achievement of the objective difficult, what characteristics will facilitate its achievement. After stating your objectives, the information you should have in your review of the market might include:

Size of market and its trends. Here you should analyse what is actually happening and has happened. It is the ideal time, after showing what you expect to sell next year, to state what you will sell in the current year, which is usually about two-thirds over at the time when such plans are presented.

Consumer profile, buying habits, geographic and socio-economic breakdown. This is the correct place to put in such basic research as you have.

Price structure. This should cover both your own and the competition's pricing and should cover the actual pricing in the market as far as you can estimate it – ie how much product sold at what sort of discount – as well as simply reprinting price lists.

Main brands in the market and their shares. Again, if you have research information put it in, if not estimate and explain the limits of your estimate.

Expenditure levels, positioning of competitors. Your own product's strengths and weaknesses, positioning, share, expenditure level.

Expected developments in the coming year. This brief outline of marketing planning cannot of course tell you what strategies to develop. But your answer to the problems and opportunities you have identified above should form the next section, refined into clear strategies. Perhaps it is sensible here to point to a few basics of marketing thinking:

1. Your first priority is always to hold on to the business you have.
2. Your second priority is to grow the business profitably.
3. You should always have a project which can potentially produce a dramatic sales breakthrough – a repositioning to exploit a usage area with much greater potential volume, an important product improvement or some other such project.
4. When you have identifed such a project you should plan an affordable test for it with clear criteria for judging its success and incorporate this in your recommendation.
5. You should always have a not-too-painful way of reducing expenditure if sales fail to perform as expected.
6. If a particular market development is likely – the introduction of a major competitor, for instance – then have a worked-out reaction ready.

The point of all this is to avoid the weakness of many plans, where the planner puts all his eggs in one basket and all his money on one eventuality, so that when the future actually happens, no room for manoeuvre is available. Things never turn out exactly as we expect. The wise planner has a way ready to exploit unexpected success and a way to limit unexpected failure.

CHAPTER 35

How to Get Good Value and Good Service

Anybody who finds themselves controlling an advertising budget will also find themselves dealing, at various times, with such specialised suppliers as photographers, finished artists, layout artists, copywriters, film companies, video companies, promotion agencies, advertising agencies, media representatives, printers and dozens of others too numerous to mention.

The same person will also not infrequently be heard to complain at the cost of producing advertising.

Cost effectiveness is important, simply because the smaller your budget the larger that percentage of it which is likely to be spent on the production of advertising materials and ideas, and consequently the smaller the percentage spent on showing the finished advertisements to the customer. If you can increase cost-effectiveness it is tantamount to increasing your budget.

This said, many people who buy advertising often seem bent on making sure the whole exercise costs them as much as it possibly can. It is possible to buy economically and it is not achieved simply by bargaining suppliers into the ground. Let us see some simple ways you can save sizeable amounts.

Plan well ahead

You can usually negotiate a better price for any job if you allow the supplier to fit it into his work pattern rather than insisting it be done tomorrow. Most suppliers are small companies or independents and their charges often seem high until you realise that they reflect the instability and rush that many of *their* clients have brought into the business.

If you insist on doing things in a rush you will pay for it. Not only will overtime and weekend work usually cost two to three times as much, there will be the alarming additional costs – sending everything everywhere by motorbike, having to re-order type because it has been ordered in the rush over the telephone, paying for expensive changes because there has been no time to proof-read.

Always get quotes in advance

There is nothing wrong with asking for a quote ahead of the job, and, if it is a sizeable assignment, asking for two or three competitive quotes. You will be surprised at the spread they often cover.

Pay promptly

Most suppliers are constantly being kept waiting for payment. If you pay promptly and without question – but make it clear that you expect fair prices – then you will usually get them.

Plan artwork for multiple use

It happens all the time. An expensive photograph is produced and used in an advertisement. And for the next advertisement virtually the same photograph has to be shot again because a different colour background is required or a slightly different angle. With careful planning the two shots could have been shot at the same time for the cost of just a little more than one. When you order artwork that you know can be frequently used then always order it with plenty of 'meat' on it, so that in a different format you don't run out of background.

Avoid unnecessary steps

Another frequent occurrence: a photographer will shoot a major shot for you and deliver perhaps 20 original transparencies almost all of which are virtually identical. You will pick one to use – and then make a dozen duplicates of that one to go to a dozen different magazines. You could have supplied them all with the originals you have mouldering in the back of a drawer unused.

Don't change your mind

Changing the contents of an ad after it has been produced or of a television commercial after it has been shot is always massively expensive. Don't set the copy till you're sure the copy is final.

Allow for changes in advance

Sometimes there are changes in the offing, and you can be fairly certain that they will have to be made. If such a situation is coming up – for instance, if you know that a change to the packaging is planned, or that a particular claim may well be attacked by a competitor and have to be changed – then allow for it. It is not a lot more expensive to shoot a film with two different packages. It is easy to record more than one sound version. It may be wise to shoot the film so that a particular phrase is not lip-sync if you are certain that that phrase may need changing in the future.

Have clear contractual arrangements

Always buy the complete copyright of any artwork, any film, any photograph, any design work you may commission. It can be very troublesome to have to reshoot simply because of some unclear point in this area – and very expensive if you simply go ahead thinking you own it.

Avoid one-offs, plan big batches

One reason why 'one measly little picture' ends up costing so much is because the photographer had to spend a full day shooting it. The client didn't arrive till nearly 11 o'clock, the background that had been prepared had to be changed and then they finally decided on a totally different angle to the one in the layout. Given this sort of record (which is all too common), most suppliers plan a full day for the simplest shot. They know that the couple of hours left over will be useless anyway.

However, if the shot is part of a comparatively large package, lasting several days and negotiated at an all-in price, it will generally work out considerably cheaper. Most suppliers like big, reliable jobs and dislike troublesome one-offs. Collect your production needs into a few big batches and you can save a mint.

Part of the same principle is not to fragment jobs. A simple brochure may require the services of a finished artist, a photographer, a copywriter, a typesetter, a lettering artist, a printer. Do not hire them all yourself. Give the job to one supplier and let him supervise the whole thing. Not only will you probably save money, you will also save hours explaining the same thing to different people and then trying to fit together the individual pieces for which nobody (except you!) is responsible.

Hold PPMs

A PPM – a pre-production meeting – is standard practice in planning a film shoot and is necessary because shooting a film is complex and expensive. However, even the simplest photographic shoot, or any other job can benefit from a pre-production meeting. It saves time because the right props are there, the model has the right clothes, the home economist has been booked and has done her work in advance.

Always insist on detailed prices

In a major project like a shoot for a TV commercial, which can easily run into many thousands, insist on a detailed breakdown of costs. While it is not recommended to then argue about each and every item, such a breakdown does show where the big costs are and enables one to examine ways of saving money – perhaps by simplifying or omitting some item which seemed a good idea before one realised how expensive it was going to be.

Always negotiate media prices

Whereas media rate cards used to be regarded as akin to Holy Writ, today they are generally understood to be no more than a basis for discussion. Here the general rule of planning well ahead may not always be right. Media hate to have blank spaces and being ready to snap up a space unit that has just become available can often get you some sharp buys. Perhaps the best advice is to dispose of your budget as much as possible well in advance, to get the maximum bargaining effect, but also to have a small reserve for special buys.

Negotiate professional services on a long-term basis

Consultant professionals and advertising agents are also very expensive if hired by the day or the hour. Their costs are reckoned on the basis that they will have to suffer a lot of wheel-spinning and idle time. Finding the people you can work with and then negotiating a fair price on the basis of a consistent amount of work is advantageous to both sides. It is also good business for you, since only someone who understands your business can make a worthwhile contribution to it. And such understanding cannot be built overnight.

Glossary

It may seem somewhat pretentious to give a book on advertising a glossary like a learned work. The fact remains, however, that the field is full of jargon, a lot of which is used imprecisely. To avoid author and reader talking at cross purposes, this modest collection of definitions may have its use.

animatic
A filmed storyboard with limited movement intended to give an impression of the finished commercial for research purposes.

awareness
The extent to which the public knows and can mention a specific company or brand. Can be further defined as **spontaneous awareness** (in answer to the question: Can you name any brands of coffee?) and **prompted awareness** (in answer to the question: Have you heard of Maxwell House?)

baseline
A line of copy summing up the advertising argument and usually placed along the bottom of the ad – hence the name.

brand
A branded product is often simply called a 'Brand' – hence 'Brand Manager' – the marketing manager responsible for a particular brand.

budget
The sum of money appropriated for advertising or marketing purposes.

campaign
A planned volume of advertising addressed to a specific aim and covering a specific period.

caption
A fugitive from the news desk, this word means a short legend written beneath a picture and describing that picture.

claim
A line of copy that encapsulates what the product claims to offer consumers – it is used primarily for functional type products where performance of a quantifiable nature can be 'claimed'.

copy
This word has two meanings – first it means the words in a press advertisement or any advertisement. However it can also mean the total

	advertisement – a brand's copy is the advertising that is used by that brand.
copy strategy	A document describing the communication aims of a campaign.
creative	Apart from its function as a term of praise or abuse, this long-suffering word has its most legitimate use in describing the less quantifiable elements in an advertising campaign – primarily copy and art.
direct mail	In this medium the advertising message is sent to the prospective customer through the post. The actual advertisement – which can consist of a brochure, a letter and perhaps a reply-paid card, for instance, is called a mail shot.
distribution	A key measurement in marketing, it defines how many retail outlets stock and sell the product. Distribution is expressed as a percentage, 100 per cent being perfect (and unattainable). Since, for instance, 20 per cent of grocery outlets account for some 80 per cent of sales, it is also important to distinguish between **unweighted distribution**, the simple percentage of outlets stocking the product, and **weighted distribution**, which expresses the percentage of the trade in that particular category which is transacted by the outlets that stock the product.
execution	Often used to make a distinction from strategy, this word describes elements in a campaign which are not of central and enduring importance and can therefore vary from subject to subject and campaign to campaign.
headline	Again, originally an editor's term, a headline is usually the largest writing in an ad, and has the function of attracting the reader into the advertisement.
impact	A favourite demand of people who are not sure of exactly what they want, it means the ability of an advertisement to attract attention and get itself noticed.
layout	A fairly detailed mounted drawing representing the finished advertisement and aiming to show how the finished advertisement will appear.

marketing	The overall title of the business activities that aim to bring goods (and services) and customers together profitably. Advertising is a part of marketing.
me-too	A popular term for a product which is consciously modelled on a successful competitor and offers no significant advantages except perhaps a lower price.
mechanic	Used of sales promotion, it implies the way in which the benefit offered stimulates the purchase of the goods.
media	In the broadest sense, anything which may contain an advertisement – TV is a medium as are newspapers, radio, magazines and so on.
message	One of many terms that describe the essential content of an advertisement.
Nielsen	Usually refers to data derived from the regular store sales audits of the A C Nielsen Company.
noting	In copy research this means seeing an advertisement without necessarily going any further and reading it or parts of it.
outdoor	An alternative name for the medium of posters.
positioning	The long-term character of a product, as defined by its function, its characteristics, the nature of the company that produces it and the consumers who typically use it.
presenter	The person in a TV commercial who appears on camera and speaks to the audience, usually representing the advertiser's viewpoint.
private label	Goods which are offered by a shop under its own brand name rather than a manufacturer's name – such as Marks & Spencer's 'St Michael' label.
product	This word can often be very broadly used, meaning, as it does, that product (or often service or even idea or viewpoint) that the advertisement aims to sell.
production	The process of progressing an approved advertisement through to a form in which it can be published.
promotion	Unlike advertising which seeks to persuade people of a product's virtues, a promotion uses another (often short-term) stimulus such as a price reduction or a free gift to achieve sales. Obviously the two can be (and are) frequently combined.
prospect	Originally a salesman's word, it identifies the

	person we mean to sell to.
recall	A term used in research to describe the memory a person has of an advertisement (usually a TV commercial). It can be expressed statistically – the percentage of viewers who remember a particular commercial or particular points in it means a recall of x per cent.
slice-of-life	A technique used in television and also in radio in which a short playlet is used to dramatise the product's message. Slice-of-life is usually in a mundane setting using characters who represent typical consumers.
slogan	A recurrent motto, usually of a memorable nature, used by a product in advertising. But see **claim, headline, baseline, strapline.**
squared-up	Pictures in an ad that are rectangular in shape and show some of the background as against those which have been cut out to show, for example, the head alone.
storyboard	The equivalent of a layout for a TV commercial, a storyboard breaks down the film into individual pictures with their attendant commentary attached, typically up to a dozen pictures for a 30-second spot.
strapline	A term used for the closing line in a commercial or advertisement, like a baseline. The origin of the phrase is in the concept of it holding the campaign together.
subhead	Short for 'sub-headline'. Whereas a headline tops the whole ad, a subhead covers a paragraph or a section.
super	Words of a commercial that appear written on the screen, instead of just being spoken.
testimonial	A statement, written or, in broadcast media, often spoken, by some independent person expressing their approval of the product.
title	See: **super.**
voiceover	In distinction to actors playing a part in a commercial or a presenter who appears on camera, this describes the Godlike disembodied voice in a commercial whose owner is never seen.

Bibliography

Advertising Works 1, 2 & 3: Papers from the IPA Effectiveness Awards. 1980, 1982, 1984. Holt, Rinehart & Winston.

Advertising Made Simple. Frank Jefkins, 1982. Heinemann.

Advertising – What It Is and How To Do It. Roderick White, 1980. McGraw Hill.

The Compleat Copywriter. Hanley Norins, 1966. McGraw Hill, USA.

Confessions of an Advertising Man. David Ogilvy, 1963. Dell, USA.

Consumer Product Development. Roderick White, 1973. Longman.

The Craft of Copywriting. Alastair Crompton, 1979. Business Books.

Creative Advertising. Charles L Whittier, 1955. Holt, Rinehart & Winston Inc., USA.

Effective Advertising. H C Carter, 1986. Kogan Page.

Madison Avenue USA. Martin Mayer, 1958. Bodley Head.

Making Ads Pay. John Caples, 1957. Harper, USA.

Marketing Mistakes. Robert F Hartley, 1986. John Wiley & Sons.

Motivation in Advertising. Pierre Martineau, 1956. McGraw Hill, USA.

Offensive Marketing. J H Davison, 1972. Cassell.

On the Writing of Advertising. Walter Weir, 1960. McGraw Hill, USA.

Positioning. Ries & Trout, 1981. McGraw Hill, USA.

Reality in Advertising. Rosser Reeves, 1961. Macgibbon & Kee.

Scientific Advertising. Claude Hopkins, 1968. Macgibbon & Kee.

Spending Advertising Money. Broadbent & Jacobs, 1984. Business Books.

The Wheel of Marketing. A C Nielsen, 1976. Published privately by A C Nielson, USA.

Index